DATE DUE

DEMCO 38-296

THE NATIONAL
ELECTRONIC LIBRARY

The National Electronic Library

A GUIDE TO THE FUTURE FOR LIBRARY MANAGERS

Edited by
Gary M. Pitkin

THE GREENWOOD LIBRARY MANAGEMENT COLLECTION
Gerard B. McCabe, *Series Adviser*

GREENWOOD PRESS
Westport, Connecticut • London

The National Electronic
Library

Library of Congress Cataloging-in-Publication Data

The National Electronic Library : a guide to the future for library
  managers / edited by Gary M. Pitkin.
     p.   cm.—(The Greenwood library management collection, ISSN
0894–2986)
    Includes bibliographical references (p.   ) and index.
    ISBN 0–313–29613–8 (alk. paper)
    1. Library information networks—United States.   2. Libraries—
United States—Special collections—Databases.   3. Digital
libraries—United States.   4. Academic libraries—United States.
5. Research libraries—United States.   I. Pitkin, Gary M.
II. Series.
Z674.8.N43   1996
021.6'5—dc20   95–40028

British Library Cataloguing in Publication Data is available.

Library of Congress Catalog Card Number: 95–40028
ISBN: 0–313–29613–8
ISSN: 0894–2986

First published in 1996

Greenwood Press, 88 Post Road West, Westport, CT 06881
An imprint of Greenwood Publishing Group, Inc.

Printed in the United States of America

The paper used in this book complies with the
Permanent Paper Standard issued by the National
Information Standards Organization (Z39.48–1984).

10 9 8 7 6 5 4 3 2 1

Copyright Acknowledgment

The editor and publisher are grateful for permission to reproduce portions of
the following copyrighted material:

David Pearce Snyder, ''Comments on the Draft Strategic Plan for Public
Libraries,'' plan submitted to the director of the Montgomery County
Department of Public Libraries, November 30, 1994.

Contents

Introduction: Issues and Concerns

Gary M. Pitkin

The purpose of this book is to focus attention on "what we have been, what we are, and what we need to be." The "we" is defined as both libraries and librarians, and the process of examining the past and the present for the purpose of a successful future is defined as "transformation." According to Kilmann and Covin, transformation "is serious, large-scale change that demands new ways of perceiving, thinking, and behaving, by all members of the organization" (Kilmann and Covin 1988: xiii–xiv).

As a reference guide for library professionals, this volume examines the historical and theoretical background of the National Electronic Library to determine what we have been and to assess where we are. The guide then uses that background to help librarians formulate what we need to be and how to engage in a successful transformation to reach that goal.

The motivations for and contents of this volume are presented through the following questions and quotations that are particularly important to the "transforming" culture of libraries based on a rapidly changing financial, political, and technological agenda:

1. *Is the library an enduring institution*? Brian L. Hawkins, in his call for a National Electronic Library, decries that

[the] urgent financial crisis of our libraries makes it clear that the traditional library will not scale into the next decade. A National Electronic Library would not only bring

significant new functionality but would address and resolve the economic issues that are fast eroding the viability of the traditional library. (Hawkins 1994: 17)

Librarian of Congress James H. Billington echoes Hawkins by stating that

[the] great temples that brought a measure of unity through enlightenment out of all our diversity—our public schools and libraries, including the Library of Congress—are in many ways dying through a slow budgetary suffocation that no one seems to notice much or mention. (Billington 1994: 254)

This apathy, as noted by Billington, is dangerous to the preservation and future of the human record. "Libraries are a link in the human chain that connects what happened yesterday with what might take place tomorrow." As enduring institutions, "libraries can and should be the base camp for the pursuit of truth and for the discovery of the new truth we will need to be making in all kinds of ways in the Information Age." As for the curators of the enduring library, "librarians are the guardians of an institution central to the American Dream, where knowledge can slowly ripen into wisdom and occasionally break through to new creativity" (Billington 1994: 267).

2. *Are libraries as buildings necessary?* A highly publicized statement by Barry Munitz (chancellor of the 22-campus California State University System) regarding the new Monterey Bay site builds a case against the library as a building. "Why bother wasting all that money on bricks and mortar and expensive tomes when it could be better spent on technology for getting information via computer? You simply don't have to build a traditional library these days" (Hafner 1995: 62).

In describing the 24-hour library, Reva Basch tends to support Munitz by stating that we are creating the "ultimate virtual library—the paperless, unlimited bandwidth, universally-accessible one we've been hearing about for years." In the 24-hour library, "seventy percent of all requests can be answered through electronic sources" (Basch 1994: 36, 38). Neither the building nor the curator/librarian appear to be necessary.

Hawkins takes a more expansive view in terms of the library no longer being just a building.

The legacy of libraries for the twenty-first century must of necessity include bricks and mortar, but also must focus on the storage of and access to information in a variety of formats, transmitted electronically. . . . We need to realize that a library is not a place and is about much more than books. (Hawkins 1994: 27, 46)

3. *What is the National Electronic Library?* Hawkins conceptualizes the National Electronic Library as replacing the traditional library as a building. The National Electronic Library is

both a solution to the economic problems facing libraries and a vehicle for a new functionality that promises to transform scholarship and bring the cultural, social and economic benefits of information to many ... specifically, what is being proposed is a collection of information, in many formats, stored electronically in locations throughout the world, but organized and collected and shared via a central networked organization. (Hawkins 1994: 24, 27)

The Library of Congress endorses the establishment of a National Electronic Library through working in concert with "the library community" to create

a National Digital Library, a virtual library that provides in electronic form a large portion of the resources of the libraries of America and that has established the standards and procedures fitting the revolutionary new world of information and librarianship. (Library of Congress 1994: 5)

The Library of Congress will assist in the creation of such a national entity by (1) enriching the existing telecommunications network, (2) creating digitized documents, (3) defining a strategic digital plan, and (4) helping lay the groundwork for the National Information Infrastructure (Billington 1994: 258).

4. *How does content relate to the National Information Infrastructure (NII)?* The Library of Congress and, through its leadership, the national library community, is actively "enriching the existing telecommunications network" and is "helping lay the groundwork for the National Information Infrastructure." What is in actuality being created? Is the content of the information superhighway going to be knowledge-based? "It is the industries, and particularly the entertainment industry, that will provide the content, filling the networks with movies, video games, shopping services, general news, and banking services" (Hawkins 1994: 19).

The library community, on the other hand, is working very hard to create an NII that will greatly facilitate the delivery of knowledge to the American public. Hawkins believes that knowledge-based content is secondary at best.

When one looks at the institutions that would provide the promised content for this technology, it is easy to see that there are crucial differences between the commercial and academic "industries." Commercial and entertainment services ... have existing organizations and the capital in place to make such new adventures viable. On the other hand, the 3,200+ college and university libraries, which operate as independent organizations offering duplicative services, possess none of the requisite capital, organizational structures, or corporate culture necessary to move effectively into the new world. (Hawkins 1994: 19–20)

Libraries and librarians can be successful in meeting the challenges imposed by these very real questions only if they embrace the transforming environment and develop new ways of perceiving, thinking, and behaving. This book focuses on where we have been, where we are, and what we need to be in terms of success in the electronic environment. Within the context of transformation and the impending concept of the National Electronic Library, the contributors address:

1. The library as an enduring institution
2. The necessity of libraries as buildings
3. The realities of the National Electronic Library
4. Content and the National Information Infrastructure

To this end, the concept of the National Electronic Library is defined and analyzed in terms of consortia, academic institutions, the public enterprise, and library education. Facilities in this electronic environment are delineated from the viewpoint of library administrators and architects. Traditional services, in terms of collection development and public and technical services, are analyzed according to what must change, what must stay the same, and what we will be doing in the very near future as a result of the transforming, electronic environment. This is followed by an examination of the relationship of strategic planning to the allocation of resources to ensure future success. A concluding chapter summarizes the entire volume by determining, "Are Libraries Necessary in the Revolutionized Environment?" Enjoy!

REFERENCES

Basch, Reva. 1994. "The 24-Hour Library." *Searcher* (September): 34–39.
Billington, James H. 1994. "Electronic Content and Civilization's Discontent." In *Technologies for the 21st Century: Content and Communication*, ed. Martin Greenberger. Santa Monica, CA: Council for Technology and the Individual.
Hafner, Katie. 1995. "Wiring the Ivory Tower." *Newsweek* (January 30): 62–63, 66.
Hawkins, Brian L. 1994. "Creating the Library of the Future: Incrementalism Won't Get Us There!" *Serials Librarian* 24, no. 3/4: 17–47.
Kilmann, Ralph H., and Teresa J. Covin. 1988. "Preface." In *Corporate Transformation: Revitalizing Organizations for a Competitive World*, ed. Ralph H. Kilmann and Teresa J. Covin. San Francisco: Jossey-Bass.
Library of Congress. 1994. *Strategic Directions Toward a Digital Library*. Washington, DC: Library of Congress.

I

The National Electronic Library

1

The National Electronic Library: The Environment Personified

Joy Reed Hughes and Karyle S. Butcher

THESIS

Two critical functions of the library are in danger of extinction: providing access to information and preserving knowledge for future generations. Only the development of the National Electronic Library has the potential to save these functions. While many libraries are engaged in relatively small-scale electronic projects, most libraries have not yet accepted the need to reallocate substantial portions of their budgets to fund the collaborative efforts needed to overcome the many significant roadblocks to building the National Electronic Library.

THREATS TO THE MISSION

Decreasing Access to Information

The library is becoming less and less able to provide access to the information needed by its customers. The rising cost of materials is one factor, but an even more important cause is the information explosion, which has made it almost impossible for any library to acquire and find space for the full range of offerings of interest to those whom the library is supposed to serve.

A Mellon Foundation report investigated the situation with respect to research libraries. These libraries account for 40 percent of the library materials purchased by academic libraries and for the majority of interlibrary loans made to nonresearch libraries. The report noted "the ever-expanding size of the universe of published materials and the rapidly increasing prices of these materials," and it expressed concern that

pressure on acquisitions budgets will cause various research libraries to look more and more alike over time, as each ceases to purchase as many of the more esoteric publications and chooses rather to be sure that essential volumes are acquired. The consequences could be a decline in the richness of collections overall, not merely a decline in the range of holdings of any one library. (Cummings et al. 1992: 3)

Another concern in this increasingly globally interdependent world is the growing inability of libraries to provide access to foreign materials. In a report to the nation's college and university presidents, the Higher Education Resource Alliance warned, "From 1980 to 1990, worldwide book production increased by 45 percent . . . [yet, there has been] an aggregate decline in the number of foreign titles acquired by both ARL [Association of Research Libraries] libraries and the Library of Congress" (1994: 3).

Perhaps the most compelling "wake-up call" the library profession has received was sounded by Brian Hawkins when he illustrated with charts and graphs how, each year, our libraries are becoming less and less able to fulfill the cornerstone of their mission—providing access to the full range of materials of interest to their customers. Hawkins's trend analyses indicate that "by the year 2001, the combined impact of inflation and the growth of information would result in our libraries being able to purchase 2 percent of the total information acquired only two decades before" (1994: 22).

Let us pause and think about Hawkins's warning. What does it mean in real terms? Suppose you work in a college library, and one of the college's strengths is its history department. Suppose also that in the early 1980s, you were able to purchase all of the books and serials requested by the history faculty.

We know that in 1994 the buying power of your acquisitions budget is less than 60 percent of what it was in 1980. So, even if the publishing numbers had held constant, you would not be able to acquire 40 percent of the materials desired by your history faculty. However, the publishing numbers have not held constant; they have increased dramatically. These dollars are purchasing less than 5 percent of the content universe you would have purchased in 1980. No wonder the faculty and graduate students complain, "the library never has what I want."

Decreased Preservation of Knowledge

The library is also becoming less able to fulfill its historic and singular role of preserving knowledge. Much of the information needed by customers is not finding its way to the libraries. The Higher Education Resource Alliance report to presidents noted, "individual researchers and scholars are putting out masses of information on electronic networks, bypassing traditional systems altogether and raising questions about the centuries-old roles of publishers and libraries" (1994: 2).

Entire disciplines have decided that their publishing future does not include a significant role for libraries. Burton Richter, president of the American Physical Association (APS), articulates his preferred future.

Any physicist, any place in the country, can turn on his computer and for free browse through the table of contents of any APS journal. Next, this browser can select those things about which he wants to see an abstract, and then, after deciding what he might read, ask for the article itself and eventually pay for it like you pay your telephone bill. (Taubes 1993: 1246)

This vision has already been realized with respect to preprints of articles. The electronic bulletin board created by Paul Ginsparg in August 1991

can be accessed from almost anywhere through electronic mail. Physicists can submit preprints . . . or they can scan a list of the preprints already on the system, read any abstracts that sound interesting, and then request that an entire preprint be transmitted, which takes a second or so and is free of charge.

Physicists report that the bulletin board has become the primary means of sharing information in their field. "By now, subscribers to one or more of the Los Alamos bulletin boards number more than 8,000, and physicists are submitting almost 600 preprints a month" (Taubes 1993: 1246).

Note that there is no mention of preserving knowledge either in the APS vision or in today's reality as exemplified by the preprint bulletin board. On my own campus, we see more and more scientists publishing "on the Net." In a few departments, we see as much time and intelligence put into the development of networked databases of research results as used to be put into writing for publication. The "middle men" (publisher and librarian) have been eliminated and information now flows directly from the creator to the consumer, perhaps to be lost forever to future generations.

There has been a shift in how people acquire information, from the book, to the radio, to the television, to the electronic network. Libraries preserve information that is published in books. An ever-increasing percentage of information is not published in books, leading to the situation described by Douglas Van Houwelin, Vice-Provost for Information Technology at the University of Michigan: "Almost nowhere in our society are people focusing on the preservation of information. . . . Libraries have focused primarily on preservation of artifacts carrying information, not on preservation of the information itself" (1993: 11). The growing amount of information that is being produced in a form that does not fit the library's preservation model is just not being preserved.

Are We in Denial?

We have painted a dismal picture—first, a picture in which our libraries become less and less important to citizens seeking current information because we are acquiring such a small percentage of that information; next, a picture where we cannot even justify the library's existence on the grounds that it is preserving the nation's cultural heritage because libraries are actually becoming, in the words of the law librarian at the Library of Congress, "archives of books not important enough to be included in databases" (Price 1993: 58).

The picture has been painted largely by using the words of a variety of leaders in our profession, leaders who lecture, write, lead symposia, and otherwise seek to educate us about the challenges we face. Knowing how often and in how many venues we have been warned, one would think that our libraries would be filled with people exhorting us to act immediately to change this "ghost of library future." One would expect the library staff and the friends of the library to be sending letters to the library administration warning, "You'd better get busy on these problems or we will all be out of a job."

These are not the kinds of letters we receive. What we get in the mail are passionate defenses of the card catalog, usually accompanied by the *New Yorker* article on that topic. I get missives explaining why the book is more valuable than any digital version, usually ending with, "No computer will ever replace the comfort of curling up with a paperback novel." And when I engage in discussions about the amount of information now provided directly to consumers via the network, people respond too often with, "That stuff on the Internet, it's disorganized junk," "Sure, the science people are bypassing the library, but they never used the library anyway," or "People will always want to come to the library and see 'real' people" (Baker 1994: 64–86).

It is not that there are no innovative people in the library using and teaching about the Internet, establishing multimedia labs, and managing CD-ROM networks. There are many. They are only allowed by their colleagues to make changes on the margins, while the bulk of the human and financial resources of the library are used to house and protect a collection that is becoming less and less relevant to the library's constituencies.

People who have studied the change process call this stage of change "denial." However, we have been in denial for ten years. It is time to move on or to risk the profession becoming so marginalized that it will no longer have any influence in the struggle for the free flow of information, for universal access, and for the preservation of information.

STRATEGIES TO PRESERVE THE MISSION

So what can we do to overcome these threats to the library's critically important mission? First, we need to create a genuine sense of urgency in our libraries, an acceptance of the fact that we are rapidly losing the ability to provide access to information and to preserve information for future generations.

There are data we can share that show that more and more people from all disciplines are getting their information off the network rather than coming to the library. Time is the one resource that most Americans lack, and they are increasingly less willing to spend it on fruitless trips to a library which contains only 5 percent of the material they need.

Second, we need to create a sense of the possible by educating ourselves and our staffs about the real revolutions taking place in the provision of electronic information.

In research labs today, for example, scientists are testing computers that have the look and feel of a paperback book. Vendors are offering intelligent cyber-knots that retrieve, filter, and organize information according to the user's preferences, and these systems will get better and better.

Third, we need to educate ourselves and our staffs about the various proposals to create a National Electronic Library, and the collaborative efforts we will all need to make to overcome the challenges to the National Electronic Library vision. We must do this not because we prefer computers to books (which we don't), but because the National Electronic Library is our best hope for preserving our missions of access to and preservation of information.

THE NATIONAL ELECTRONIC LIBRARY

Functions

How could a National Electronic Library assist us in providing access to and preserving information? (1) It could provide support to libraries to digitize unique materials and link these with the National Electronic Library; (2) it could facilitate sharing of the burden of digitizing common collections, thus decreasing duplication of effort; (3) it could negotiate national contracts for high-use, commercially published items; and (4) it could serve as a clearinghouse for shareware which enable electronic library services, such as an electronic interlibrary loan or reference service via interactive video.

The National Electronic Library could develop systems to locate, evaluate, and catalog material published on the Internet; it could provide guidance to librarians on how to catalog locally produced electronic materials, including research databases and multimedia objects, so that these can be easily retrieved and used in other contexts; and it could provide guidance to universities seeking to publish scholarly material electronically, including coordinating the peer review and archival processes.

These are among the various functions proposed for a National Electronic Library. The proposals differ in their vision of how such a system would be organized and funded, who it would serve, and what types of collaboration would be required.

Models for a National Electronic Library

The Brian Hawkins Model

The Hawkins model calls for a nonprofit corporation to manage and obtain resources for the National Electronic Library. It relies heavily on voluntary digitization of materials and voluntary "fair share" access fees from institutions. (One suggestion he makes is a tithe of 10 percent of a library's acquisitions budget.) The digitized collections, including multimedia documents, would be stored locally but managed by the central organization. Access to the materials would be free to the individual user.

The first goal of Hawkins's National Electronic Library (HNEL) is to "meet the needs of scholars, collecting and preserving those things not likely to be collected or held in other resources" (1994: 30). A primary strategy of the HNEL would be to change the scholarly publishing paradigm for serials by "providing a coherent and stable environment for electronic publishing to flourish" (1994: 41). He also expects the HNEL to select or develop technical standards and searching tools.

In addition to research libraries, the HNEL's collaborative partners would include some publishers, those that are able to function in and make marketable contributions to the electronic world. The HNEL would work with publishers to create and test models for national and international site licenses. Business relationships with organizations such as Research Libraries Group and Online Computer Library Center (OCLC) are also part of the plan.

Among the unique aspects of the Hawkins proposal is its emphasis on social engineering. Instead of proposing changes in the copyright laws, he proposes tax incentives for companies that donate electronic information and a change in the rules concerning valuation of publishing inventory.

His proposal also stands out because of its emphasis on a lean and dynamic organizational structure which he contrasts to the semi-paralysis existing in most universities and membership organizations due to their consensus mode of making decisions.

There are several questions, however, that need to be raised about the model. These include the lack of a plan for the cataloging of research databases despite the focus on the needs of research libraries; the lack of a plan for coordinated collection development and management; the lack of comprehensive solutions to the conflict between the desire of libraries to provide free information and the desire of publishers (and some authors) to make a profit.

The Library of Congress Model

The Library of Congress (LC) model is referred to as the National Digital Library. This model proposes a more centralized electronic library with most of the digitized material housed at the Library of Congress. The model proposes to digitize "large numbers of resource materials that are now available only to researchers who must visit reading rooms of the library," and "a wider range of its unique holdings, such as audio and video materials, the contents of books that cannot leave the Library on interlibrary loan, and one-of-a-kind manuscript materials" (1994: 2). An LC goal is to have 5 million LC items digitized by the year 2000.

LC also proposes to provide leadership in the location, organization, and preservation of nontraditional electronic resources. It has several committees in place "investigating ways for the Library to identify, download, service, and preserve the journals of permanent research value and in digital form available over the Internet" (1994: 11).

The LC proposal recognizes the importance of developing standards for cataloging and preserving electronic information. And it proposes to develop new services to assist people in accessing and efficiently utilizing the electronic collections.

Among its collaborative partners would be other libraries which would provide expertise and materials, corporate leaders who could provide funding and technical expertise, and copyright users and owners. The latter would "formulate pilot projects that address the copyright and intellectual property issues that are becoming prominent in the digital environment, including collective licensing mechanisms" (1994: 3).

There is little doubt that LC has the capability to undertake and carry out large digitization projects, particularly when there is external funding for the project. There is more than a little skepticism, however, concerning the ability of LC to overcome negative aspects of its organizational culture. Skepticism is based on the length of time it takes LC to make decisions and then incorporate them into practice. This inhibits its ability to succeed in a transformational event of such magnitude as the creation of a National Electronic Library.

As described by LC's law librarian,

Our "electronic library" consists of a series of individual projects as basic as the installation of local area networks and as advanced as the multimedia American Memory Project. All of these must be overlaid onto an institution like [many of yours] in which staffs are stressed by too much strategic planning without practical results, increasingly demanding patrons, and static or dwindling resources.

At LC we add an historic belief that we are the center of our own universe with challenges on a scale so large that we must custom design and implement our own systems, coupled with a broken infrastructure—a mail system so clogged that law serials are two years out-of-date; a human resource system that cannot get people on board in four to six months; a cumbersome centralized mainframe-oriented information technology group; full shelves; and arrearages. (Price 1993: 55)

Discipline and Areas Studies Models

There are other models for a national electronic library on the table, but these tend to be more discipline specific. For example, a Draft Strategic Plan (approved by the ARL Research Collections Committee in October 1994) "describes a system in which participating research libraries would share responsibility for collecting foreign imprint publications, and would function as access nodes in a 'distributed North American collection for foreign materials' " (1994: 2). The Plan also calls for coordinated collection development and management. It proposes to begin exploring electronic storage and delivery issues in three demonstration projects.

The proposed Agricultural Network Information Center (AgNIC) has some similarities with the proposal to link collections of foreign imprint materials. It, too, calls for information to be digitized and stored locally. It is much more ambitious, however, in that it intends to link seekers of information to research databases, subject area experts, courses, and extension materials, most of which are not usually cataloged or published commercially.

COLLABORATING TO OVERCOME THE BARRIERS

The Barriers

There are real and formidable barriers to the development and use of a National Electronic Library, whether that library be comprehensive or discipline specific. These barriers include:

- the lack of appropriate current copyright and site licensing regulations for a distributed, electronic environment;
- a lack of standards for the organization and retrieval of electronic information, especially multimedia and noncommercially published information;
- the inability to develop cost-effective ways to provide training to information providers, organizers, and users; and
- a lack of access to electronic information due to physical location and funding.

These are not new problems. While there may not yet exist any single, agreed-upon solutions to any of the barriers, there are people and organizations currently proposing and/or prototyping strategies to address parts of the problems. There are also organizations in place with which we could work to develop collaborative strategies.

Copyright and Site Licensing

One solution often proposed is to contract for copyright with state and regional networks. For example, national site license agreements would be established which would call for state or regional networks to make a "single, flat payment upfront, with no additional charges for normal distribution and use (as contractually defined)" (Hunter 1992: 71).

Another solution often proposed is that the universities become the publishers of scholarly information. The Association of American Universities (AAU) commissioned the report "Intellectual Properties in an Electronic Environment," which points out that in the current paradigm faculty sell or give their research to publishers who then sell it back (frequently at prohibitively high prices) to libraries. AAU recommends copyright "being held jointly by the author(s) of the work and a consortium of universities, rather than by the author and a publisher" (1994: 37).

AAU also recommends that universities develop copyright policies to govern electronic information. Some universities are indeed doing so. What is needed, though, is an organized method for sharing policy information as well as some formal way for libraries to work together in the development and testing of new policies. AAU and other consortia need to provide the leadership to make such collaborative projects happen.

The Organization of Electronic Information

A major roadblock to the creation of a National Electronic Library is the lack of standards for searching for and cataloging electronic information. Each day brings forth a new method for accessing information on the Internet. (My computer has the campus gopher, Mosaic, and Netscape on its first screen, and other choices on later screens.)

Yet, these tools are fundamentally at the "point and click" stage. If time is money, then many dollars are lost searching for directions on the information highway. If we are to provide access to the electronic library for all seekers of information, we must have a system for finding information. This system must be at least as easy and as comprehensive as the familiar on-line catalog.

Leading-edge institutions are working on projects to develop such systems. The University of Virginia's Electronic Text Center "makes an extraordinarily wide range of information available electronically—information that would normally need to be sought laboriously from far flung original sources" (Borman 1993: 18). A similar project in the sciences is the Chemistry On-line Retrieval Experiment (CORE) at Cornell University. CORE represents a collaboration among four disparate information providers: OCLC, Bell Communications Research (Bellcore), the American Chemistry Society, and Cornell University's Mann Library. California Polytechnic State University at San Luis Obispo (CalPoly) has also formed a partnership with the private sector by joining with Bellcore to "implement Superbook, an electronic document 'browser' that can deliver library materials, journal abstracts, and other documents with text, graphics, and video to the desktop via the network" (Baker and Gloster 1994: 9).

For every well-funded project, though, there are multiple nonfunded, seat-of-the-pants library projects trying to do the same thing. In each of our libraries, we have a few people struggling to understand issues related to organizing or retrieving electronic information. As a profession, we must ask ourselves if this is the best use of our staff. These local projects, no matter how impressive, do not have the power to bring about the changes libraries and librarians must experience in order to move toward a National Electronic Library.

Leadership is needed to promote collaborative projects and a shared understanding on the part of local libraries. We need to forgo the glories attendant upon developing our own projects from scratch and instead commit to more collaborative endeavors. The Coalition for Networked Information (CNI), for example, could sponsor a week-long seminar which would feature presentations and requests for support from the leading-edge projects.

Models could be presented or developed at the seminar which libraries could take back to their local or regional community for discussion and local implementation. As local libraries developed local projects congruent with a model, they would be serving to field test methods of information organization and access.

On regional levels, libraries need to come together under the auspices of their state associations or state libraries to develop regional and state projects to address barriers to information organization and retrieval. The local libraries could provide the financial or personnel assistance needed to create a regional team which would develop, adapt, or field test methods for organizing and finding electronic information.

At the national level, there is a great need for library consortium leadership to bring together libraries and the private sector to tackle sophisticated issues related to the organization and retrieval of electronic information. In a recent *American Libraries* article, Liz Bishoff from OCLC outlines projects that could be tackled on a national level through a partnership of libraries and private sector information providers:

Enduser access to full-text files on OCLC, RLG, and regional networks via America Online, Prodigy, and Compserve. . . . Joint ventures in which Regional Bell Operating Companies and cable companies would provide highways and entertainment, and libraries would provide in-home and in-business delivery information such as On-line Public Access Catalogs, local databases, gophers to regional libraries and e-mail support for information requests and finding aids. (1994: 991)

Local libraries could assist such national projects by allocating financial or staff support. In return, the local library would be allowed to have gratis or at reduced cost the fruits of the project. If enough libraries send one or two of their ''best and brightest'' to work for a year on a significant well-organized and well-funded national project, many of the barriers to the National Electronic Library would be overcome.

Training

Training people how to find information on the Internet is one of the most labor-intensive operations a library can undertake. The amount of available information is increasing daily. The lack of a common interface prohibits all but the most dedicated from learning more than a handful of databases. Moreover, some of the library's customers, such as faculty, want training on an as-needed basis rather than in prescheduled workshops.

We in library administration are all struggling with training issues, and are all investing staff resources in teaching workshops and creating course materials and documentation. Each library starts from scratch, makes similar mistakes, and then moves on to develop training for the next application. Again, leadership and collaboration are needed.

Practically every state library association has a continuing education committee. If these committees could agree to terminate programs they are currently undertaking, they could collaborate to develop basic training modules to be made available to libraries in the respective state.

The need for training will grow without bounds, however, unless we use our influence to design applications. We need to encourage and support library organizations, such as Library Orientation/Instruction Exchange, to work with vendors to provide better upfront design of electronic software and databases.

Universal Access

Universal access to networks and networked information appears to be an insurmountable challenge in a telecommunications environment that is ever more deregulated and market driven. This issue, like copyright, is one that can consume hours and hours of discussion time in a library or at a library conference, usually ending with all parties frustrated and convinced that market forces will win out over the library's historic commitment to providing information free to all.

We need to shift our vision from electronic access "at the desktop" to electronic access at a local access point (LAP). The LAP might be in a public library, a county extension office, the local high school, or a community center. The goal of providing Internet access to every home has the greatest opportunity for success when libraries work with community groups to obtain funding for and establish local access points.

At Oregon State University (OSU), a team drawn from the library, computer center, telecommunications, and media services visited the extension offices in 22 of the most rural counties to learn about their needs and resources. Initiatives are now underway to bring the Internet to several of these offices as a first step in creating county LAPs. OSU also works with small independent telephone companies, assisting them in developing the expertise to offer Internet services to their customers. And OSU is part of a wider collaborative effort known as Building Oregon's Electronic Communities (BOEC). This group is attempting to develop community support for and expertise in the development of community networks.

CHALLENGES TO COLLABORATION

Collaboration is essential to overcoming the barriers to the development and use of a National Electronic Library. And collaboration is recognized as integral to the functioning of any National Electronic Library. The call for collaboration with local libraries is evident in each of the models previously described.

All of the National Electronic Library proposals, with the exception of the Library of Congress, require materials to be acquired, digitized, and stored at the local libraries, then linked through the services of the national library. In effect, the models are asking local libraries to donate significant amounts of human and financial resources to make materials available to other libraries in the expectation that the value gained will outweigh the costs. The proposals also call, to varying degrees, for shared collection development and management decisions.

How realistic are these expectations for resource sharing and shared decision making? We know that university and library leaders are calling for such collaboration. The Higher Education Resource Alliance report of the Foreign Acquisitions Task Force recommendation stated: "Acquisitions funding must move away from the focus on self-sufficient collections and toward cooperative collection development and sharing" (1994: 3–4).

But most libraries spend only a very small portion of their budget on collaborative activities that would accelerate the electronic library vision. After a 1991 gathering of a group of Chief Academic Officers (CAOs) and Library Directors to discuss preferred futures for libraries, it was noted:

Cooperation was rarely mentioned by workshop participants as a key strategy for achieving their preferred futures. While there are a few notable instances where librarians are working with close neighbors . . . a general lack of interest in cooperation beyond the most peripheral programs was apparent. Librarians may believe cooperation has achieved success, but in the eyes of the CAOs, cooperative activities have many miles to travel, and many promises to keep before success is achieved. (Dougherty and Hughes 1991: 16)

In 1993 a similar group was assembled, this time augmented by faculty and information technology directors. The gathering revealed significant differences in strategic priorities that must be reconciled before libraries are able and willing to reallocate people and money to shared endeavors. These differences are illustrated by the different goals for the library in the year 2000 that were expressed by the groups attending the "preferred futures" meeting in 1993.

The university administrators (presidents, CAOs) attending the meeting asserted that libraries must:

provide access to information of any type anywhere; acquire rights to use, but not acquire information on speculation that it might be needed later; provide proportionately more access than ownership; . . . require no increase in total dollar share of resources spent; no increase in space; . . . establish own organization to sell scholarly output; stimulate collaboration between providers and scholars; [and] . . . not publicize number of volumes in college statistics; instead emphasize access to information that can be provided. (Dougherty and Hughes 1993: 12)

The faculty attending the 1993 "preferred futures" meeting said that libraries must:

play a more active role in scholarly communication; take over publishing function; scan texts; distribute electronic texts; [and] . . . play a more direct role in communication through discipline-oriented invisible colleges. (Dougherty and Hughes 1993: 12)

Library directors attending the meeting, though, responded differently to the challenge to define a preferred future for libraries. Although they also stressed "access" and "providing information," it was the only group that said "preserve the library as a place," and the only group that said the library needed to "continue to focus on preservation of print information sources as well as electronic sources" (Dougherty and Hughes 1993: 12).

Their hopes for the future reveal the conundrum. If libraries continue to spend most of their resources on the acquisition and preservation of print materials and continue to envision the library as "a place" where people come to get resources, they will have neither the resources nor the mental mind-set necessary to do what needs to be done to actualize the electronic library. Electronic endeavors will remain marginal.

The remedy is to reallocate substantial resources to collaborative projects that will enable the development of a National Electronic Library. To do so we must find the courage to allocate staff and money away from print collections and reallocate them to collaborative electronic library projects.

The commitment to reallocate funds and personnel resources is fostered by the belief that our libraries are not on a life-sustaining course—our libraries are becoming weaker and weaker each year, less and less able to provide access to information the customers need. Librarians are facing critical allocation choices. Shall we continue "business as usual" or do we team up with our neighbors, commit our resources to trail blazing, and risk losing everything on the journey?

REFERENCES

Association of Research Libraries. 1994. *Reports of the AAU Task Forces on Intellectual Property Rights in an Electronic Environment.* Washington, DC: Association of Research Libraries.

Association of Research Libraries, Research Collections Committee. 1994. *Draft Strategic Plan.* Unpublished document (October 19).

Baker, Nicholson. 1994. "Annals of Scholarship: Discards." *New Yorker* 70 (April 4): 64–86.

Baker, Warren J., and Arthur S. Gloster, II. 1994. "Moving Towards the Virtual University: A Vision of Technology in Higher Education." *Cause/Effect* 17, no. 2 (Summer): 4–11.

Bishoff, Liz. 1994. "Does Organizational Networking Have a Future in a Competitive Environment?" *American Libraries* (December): 990–991.

Borman, Stu. 1993. "Advances in Publishing Herald Changes for Scientists." *C&EN* (June 14): 10–24.

Cummings, A. M., M. L. Witee, W. G. Bowen, L. O. Lazarus, and R. H. Ekman. 1992. *University Libraries and Scholarly Communication.* Washington, DC: Association of Research Libraries for the Andrew W. Mellon Foundation.

Dougherty, R. M., and C. Hughes. 1991. *Preferred Library Futures.* Mountain View, CA: Research Library Group.

Dougherty, R. M., and C. Hughes. 1993. *Preferred Library Futures II: Charting the Paths.* Mountain View, CA: Research Library Group.

Hawkins, Brian L. 1994. "Creating the Library of the Future: Incrementalism Won't Get Us There!" *Serials Librarian* 24, no. 3/4: 17–47.

Higher Education Resource Alliance of ARL, CAUSE, and EDUCOM. 1994. *What Presidents Need to Know . . . about the AAU Action Agenda for University Libraries, HEIRAlliance Executive Strategies Report #5.* Boulder, CO: CAUSE.

Hunter, Karen. 1992. "The National Site License Model." *Serials Review* 18, no. 1–2 (Spring and Summer): 71–91.

Library of Congress, Digital Library Coordinating Committee. 1994. *Strategic Directions Toward a Digital Library.* Unpublished draft document (September 13).

Price, Kathleen. 1993. "Xanadu Revisited: Clothing the Emperor for the New Library Role in the Electronic Library Paradigm." In *Electronic Access to Information: A New Service Paradigm* (proceedings from a symposium held July 23–24, Mountain View, CA), pp. 51–58.

Taubes, Gary. 1993. "Publication by Electronic Mail Takes Physics by Storm." *Science* 259 (February 26): 1246–1248.

Van Houwelin, Douglas E. 1993. "Knowledge Services in the Digitized World: Possibilities and Strategies." In *Electronic Access to Information: A New Service Paradigm* (proceedings from a symposium held July 23–24, Mountain View, CA), pp. 5–16.

2

Consortia and the National Electronic Library

Alan N. Charnes

INTRODUCTION

Right now, the information highway is mostly talk and little action. The electronic library, our cherished concept related to the information highway and the subject of this chapter, also is in danger of being talked to death. The widely endorsed goal of "universal access, by students and faculty, to information in all possible media via a single multifunction workstation" (Hawkins 1994: 20) will remain just outside our grasp unless we adjust some of the existing mores and behavior patterns of the library community. We don't need a revolution. But we do need a commitment to change and a sense of urgency.

Brian L. Hawkins has done a great service. He has written a well-reasoned and provocative article which accurately describes existing conditions (Hawkins 1994: 17–47). His analysis is solid. And he is justified in sounding the alarm. His position weakens, however, when he shifts from a discussion of the problem to consideration of recommendations. Additional thought needs to be given to his proposed solution and his assertion that incrementalism can't accomplish our goal.

He argues that our best option is a nonprofit corporation charged with planning and implementing the National Electronic Library. To make his proposal work, Hawkins requests unprecedented financial support from the library community, a request that in many ways is unreasonable. He asks library administrators to voluntarily contribute 10 percent of library acquisition budgets to the national independent nonprofit corporation. To be fair, Hawkins makes it clear that the 10 percent amount is merely illustrative and the actual figure would be derived from a business plan that the corporation would develop.

But such support is unlikely to be realized. He is asking library administrators to give up both money and control. No way. Perhaps a viable nonprofit corporation option could be designed, but not without reversing the money and control recommendation.

Another unworkable recommendation is his suggestion that federal income tax incentives be offered to owners of electronic information to encourage them to contribute their property for the public good. There are many of these so-called tax expenditures in the federal tax code. History tells us that it has taken extensive and expensive lobbying to get them there. Academics and librarians simply don't have the horsepower.

For the reasons noted above and others to be discussed later, I believe that the nonprofit corporation model is unworkable. An expanded consortial model is recommended instead. The case is a simple one, and it goes as follows:

1. costs are beyond control;
2. traditional library service demands are exploding;
3. new demands such as distance and lifetime learning are continuously being made;
4. the financial crisis has been delayed, but can't be delayed any longer;
5. alternative strategies are needed to manage the financial crisis;
6. the National Electronic Library is the most promising, cost-effective alternative strategy for sharing resources;
7. librarians will control the outcome;
8. librarians work most constructively in a collegial setting; and
9. many consortia already exist, thereby expediting development through existing organizational structures.

There is enormous power in librarians working cooperatively toward a mutually beneficial result that they understand could not otherwise be achieved. The real world has placed consortia in a position to be able to actually create electronic libraries, and, if we optimize that potential, to create a national network of electronic libraries. Consortia can serve as the building blocks. Stacking those blocks together in what could be described as a consortium of consortia can produce the result we desire.

Two assumptions are being made in this chapter. One is that the National Electronic Library can't be planned and imposed from the top down. It can only grow from the bottom up and be propelled by enlightened self-interest. Even if federal funds or tithed-pooled funds could support development of a business plan and the establishment of a national pilot project, there is no willing audience. The diversity of purpose, resources, needs, and attitudes in the academic community work against an imposed result.

The other key assumption is that the free market will work against control of the electronic library by any single entity. This is not intended to be a political statement, but merely recognition of the fact that many diverse interests will share in the development of a National Electronic Library. No one group is in control. Fortunately, there is much mutual interest.

We acknowledge that librarians are the key players. They come as close as anyone can to controlling the outcome. But there are other participants who, in the give and take of the marketplace, will help to shape the final product. Library system vendors will continue to offer new and important products and services. Hardware manufacturers will build better equipment available at lower cost. School administrators, faculty, and researchers will play a role. So will authors and publishers. Cable television companies have a stake, as do state governments and regional organizations. The federal government will also participate. But none of these interest groups work in libraries every day. Librarians do, and therefore it is imperative that their voices be heard.

The missing pieces to moving ahead quickly are absence of leadership and a widespread lack of comprehension about the magnitude and urgency of the issue. Hawkins has helped us significantly on the latter. Clearly, we must move ahead now.

ANALYSIS

The subject of this chapter is consortia and the National Electronic Library. Hawkins's paper, referred to and quoted from extensively in this chapter, provides an excellent resource and a comprehensive framework for examining the issue. It is recommended reading.

But this chapter attempts to address the issue more broadly. It is difficult to know for certain if different ideas are being discussed when we hear about the National Electronic Library, the national digital library, the one-library concept, the 24–hour library, and the virtual library. No one has set about defining them in great detail. But they probably are the same or at least they are elements of a common vision. This chapter assumes that the goal of universal access to all media via one terminal is the shared vision. The discussions which follow are all about ways to make that vision a reality.

Four paths to the National Electronic Library are discussed in Hawkins's paper. Three are rejected and one, the nonprofit corporation model, is offered for implementation. My assertion is that the entertainment model, the pay-per-publication model, and the government model were undervalued and, in fact, have much to contribute toward reaching the stated goal. At the same time, the nonprofit corporation model was overvalued. But if significantly reshaped by a freshly energized and focused consortial movement, the vision can become reality.

The Entertainment Model

We all understand that, judged on the basis of intellectual content, cable TV is practically beneath contempt. As broadcast television was before it, the cable TV spectrum remains a vast wasteland of exploitive talk shows, shopping channels, and junk sports. Could there possibly be any redeeming intellectual content somewhere buried in that mess? Hawkins says "no." I say "yes." There is scholarship of a sort available today on cable TV in almost every home in the United States. Our task is to recognize its potential and upgrade its content.

In fact, the commercial interests are reaching out to us. Neither party has a good idea about how to make this connection, but the potential is there. Literally billions of dollars are looking for ways to fill 500 television channels. They may have to hold their noses, but librarians will have to find a way to work with commercial interests. The sad fact is those with money have the wrong vision and those of us who believe that we have the right vision don't have much money.

The key is interactivity. To be sure, Time Warner's recent announcement of interactive pilot projects completely misses the academic mark and, even in the commercial arena, offers pretty weak projects. Movies on demand, instant home shopping, and transcontinental card games won't cut it. But distance learning, life-long learning, and universal access, tenets of our library faith, could flourish in a dollar-rich environment.

For some academic subjects, the triad of the interactive television set, the personal computer, and the electronic gateway to library services is an unbeatable package. The electronic syllabus practically writes itself for courses in the arts, contemporary affairs, modern history, and certain hard sciences. But are the cable operators interested?

Bernard J. Luskin, President of Jones Education Networks, Global Operations and CEO of Jones Interactive, Inc., is not only interested but feels that "the education market is central to the future" (Luskin 1994: 2). His Mind Extension University (MEU) is a 24-hour, seven-day-a-week network which provides diverse programming for self-enhancement plus degree and certificate programs. MEU programming is received in 26 million homes in the United States. MEU currently maintains educational affiliations with more than 30 universities and colleges, including two which are members of the Colorado Alliance of Research Libraries.

The MEU's of the world won't be deterred. Luskin sees that "enlightened cable operators are uniquely positioned to participate in the dramatic new education initiatives. Cable is at the forefront because of the potential of immediate access and two-way transactional programming" (Luskin 1994: 7). Through a concept he calls the "smart house" which is marketing lingo for the television-PC-electronic library triad, Luskin states, "distance education represents a major future business and social opportunity" (Luskin 1994: 7).

Pay-Per-Publication Model

While the ideal of a "free" library continues to enrich our lives, the dirty secret is that someone has to pay for all this. Right now the costs are hidden. Few libraries have cash registers at the check-out desk, but every library is tied to federal, state, and local tax proceeds, tuition, fees, grants, and contributions. Hawkins guesses total U.S. library academic budgets at over $1 billion.

The pay-per-publication model is not new and I believe does no violence to the concept of a free library. That ideal can and must be maintained, limited, of course, to the availability of material in the library and at traditional service levels. Accessing material electronically, perhaps from sources outside the library, and with expedited delivery, ought to be viewed as a premier service, subject to a service charge.

Hawkins acknowledges this service in his description of the UnCover product which, in fact, does provide quick access to more than 16,000 journals, plus rapid article delivery. However, he has trouble with the concept, although he sees the UnCover idea as "an important intermediate strategy to offset some of the spiraling inflation costs" (Hawkins 1994: 33). He sees the following four problems:

1. Because access, not ownership, is being purchased, historic cooperation among libraries would end, further widening the gulf between large and small institutions.

2. Quality would not be maintained. Information available through these alternative models would not necessarily fulfill the broad range of needs which traditional research libraries have fulfilled. Commercially viable databases would not include important but infrequently used materials, such commercial ventures being driven by market considerations and not research requirements. Pay-per-publication thus is seen as incompatible with the need to preserve the knowledge of our society and the enduring values of the research library.

3. Logistical problems in setting up metering and chargeback mechanisms would absorb a great deal of time. Hawkins feels that this effort could be better spent on achieving a broader public good.

4. Pay-per-publication would create less rigorous scholarship. This is Hawkins' principal concern. He suggests that "[t]his model works against quality, against thoroughness, and is most likely to result in suboptimized use of limited research funds" (Hawkins 1994: 34).

Those all are important issues. In particular, his concern about the reduced quality of scholarship needs careful attention. None of us wants to be a party to such an occurrence. However, it is difficult to see that happening. Yes, it is true that pay-per-publication will affect the size of collections at individual institutions, and that clearly is a loss. But the more than offsetting gain is electronic access to a national library of information.

In addition, while the design of this national library is still in the future, it will surely include a traditional no-fee specification. Pay-per-publication is an additional feature, not a replacement. Serious research can be undertaken as it always has. The pay-per-publication feature is an enhancement, and for certain kinds of research presents opportunities for access to and organization of information that otherwise would not be possible.

I am a member of the Board of Directors of the UnCover Company and am strongly committed to its products. You may wish to disregard my comments here, but I believe that the pay-per-publication model works well and, judging by patron response, provides a needed service. The access versus ownership debate may still be going at high policy levels, but at the working researcher level, the debate is over.

Commitment to UnCover and similar electronic article delivery systems is a winning cost-saving strategy. It is difficult to insist on journal ownership, with its spiraling high costs, in the face of low-cost instant access and quick delivery of requested articles. Two initiatives currently underway in the Colorado Alliance are relevant. Although the motivation in each case was to save money, they also bear on the "free" service issue.

One is an experiment in free unmediated access to UnCover journal articles for students and faculty at Colorado State University. The results are encouraging. At surprisingly low cost to the library and at no cost to the patron, UnCover permits university students and faculty to receive journal articles that are not in the university's collection. The other project, based on the availability of the Colorado Alliance UnCover database, will permit library administrators to cancel journal subscriptions, confident that they know exactly how many of the partner institutions retain the journal and from whom they have received assurances of special service.

Access by subscription to on-line databases is another rapidly expanding pay-per-publication feature. There is no end to the demand and no end of vendors developing these subscription databases. Again, a Colorado Alliance example. Using consortial funds, we have acquired access to the Online Computer Library Center's (OCLC's) First-Search basic database package on behalf of all of the member libraries. We purchased a fixed number of concurrent users and fully expect that the number will have to be increased as the product reaches its full use potential.

Government Model

This is a wild card. There is some good and a lot of bad if the federal government takes a lead role in funding and managing the National Electronic Library. Even if all the political problems could be solved, building a giant system from the top down is problematic.

The literature is full of examples of failed large-scale system development projects. "Studies have shown that for every six new large-scale software systems that are put in operation, two others are canceled. The average software development project overshoots its schedule by half; large projects generally do worse. And some three quarters of all large systems are "operating failures" that either do not function as intended or are not used at all" (Gibbs 1994: 86–87).

Regrettably from my point of view, the author of that conclusion, *Scientific American*'s W. Wayt Gibbs, offers as his most vivid example of the software crisis the automated baggage system at the new Denver International Airport. I am certain that everyone knows by now about that civic embarrassment. Conceptually, the $200 million system is a no-brainer. It is mature technology successfully operated at other airports. The problems come with scaling up. There are 4,000 independent telecars running on 21 miles of steel track delivering luggage among the counters, gates and claim areas of 20 different airlines. There are 100 computers, 5,000 electric eyes, 400 radio receivers, and 56 bar-code scanners. The system is now working, but it remains as a rich example of the difficulties in government-sponsored, large-scale development.

The new congressional leadership is not likely to have much interest in funding intellectual esoterica such as a National Electronic Library. They probably will be content to limit their involvement to token financial support and to permitting the Library of Congress to continue to look for outside support for its digital library project.

This is an important project, and, if financial support can be obtained, represents movement by a government entity toward our goal. The Library of Congress intends to create a vast virtual library of digitized images of books, drawings, manuscripts, and photographs that would be sent over computer networks to computer screens and televisions all across the country. This requires the best equipment and the latest technology.

Also, a lot of money. The Digital Library Coordinating Committee currently is soliciting funds from the public and private sectors for its multi-million-dollar undertaking. Digitizing the more than 100 million items in the collection is a daunting task, particularly because a good deal of the collection is rapidly deteriorating and fragile. Library of Congress administrators have set for themselves the high goal of becoming the gateway to all significant publicly available information regardless of location or format.

Perhaps funding can be found. Although unlikely, it is possible that enough broad national interest can be developed around the issue, forcing Congress to act. There is yet another possibility. Who is to say that some clever pork-sniffing congressman won't see economic development opportunities for his home district and start beating the library drum?

Nonprofit Corporation Model

This is Hawkins's chosen route to achievement of our goal. However, he has painted an idealized picture of the independent, nonprofit corporation that he envisions will be the new National Electronic Library's "focal point for negotiations and central brokerage, eliminating unnecessary costs and duplication, leveraging resources, and promoting standards'' (Hawkins 1994: 35). He sees the organization cooperating ''with public and private institutions as a partner in the broader market in which it is a part. Such a model would have all the enormous financial and legal benefits of being a charitable entity, set up for the benefit of the broader society'' (Hawkins 1994: 35).

I am the executive director of such an organization, the Colorado Alliance of Research Libraries. The Alliance is a not-for-profit corporation registered in Colorado and recognized by the Internal Revenue Service as a 501(c)(3) corporation. It includes both public and private universities in Colorado and Wyoming and one major public library. The annual budget is set by a Board of Directors who are appointed by the university presidents, and, for the public library, by the mayor of Denver. Funding is unusual, being a combination of assessments and royalty income.

Assessments are based on a two-factor formula reflecting each member institution's bibliographic record count and the number of terminal ports in use at a particular point in time. The two factors serve as proxies for size of collection and usage, and the assessment pool is prorated accordingly.

Royalty income comes from two for-profit companies, The CARL Corporation and The UnCover Company. Both were created out of the founding, not-for-profit Colorado Alliance and although historically connected, both are independent corporations.

The point is that the Colorado Alliance is like Hawkins's nonprofit corporate model. While the model works well when sized for the Colorado Alliance and its eight institutions, it will not work well on a national scale. Even operating exactly as proposed by Hawkins, insulated from all the defects of member organizations, the corporation is just too big. Such a structure might succeed if the federal government paid all the bills and, therefore, established all the rules. Even then, it would be impossible to continuously ensure that the federal position, the library needs, and the public interest were identical.

I am arguing in support of consortia, actually a consortium of consortia, a concept that I believe will emerge naturally as time passes. Unfortunately, the emergence will be painfully slow and too much time will pass if the library community fails to fully accept its responsibilities in this matter. The National Electronic Library will not be invented. It will grow on its own as the urgency of the issue hits home. I see a national agenda shaping itself and a combination of interests forming what in effect will be a national consortium. Another way to visualize this structure is as concentric rings of partners—groups overlapping and cooperating as needed.

Hawkins wouldn't agree. He believes instead that his proposed nonprofit organization would be ''efficient and business-like.'' He states further that: ''[I]n fact, as a matter of key strategy, this non-profit corporation would be carefully structured to operate as an independent efficient business, quite unlike most of the consortia, cooperative associates and public institutions that characterize much of higher education'' (Hawkins 1994: 35). One cannot dispute his objective, but its attainment is unlikely by the scheme he proposes.

CONSORTIAL CONCERNS

While this chapter argues for consortial networking as the best way to move the national library agenda forward, the mixed record of consortial performance needs to be addressed. Even when the willingness is there, cooperation often does not happen, hindered by bureaucratic traditions of academic decision making. Hawkins correctly cautions us to be careful about hitching our wagon to the traditional member organization, which is likely to get bogged down in process and undue deliberation as it strives to achieve consensus.

But even with its limitations, the consortial approach remains the most promising. The numerous barriers to effective consortial performance will be overcome because the facts of economic life will energize the ethic of cooperation. The concerns listed below, which describe the current environment, are presented in the interest of looking at the complete picture. The assumption is that they are manageable, and, in time, will become nonissues.

1. *Competition.* Each of the institutions that we represent is different and special. Each represents years and even centuries of tradition. Institutional attributes are enthusiastically promoted in recruiting students, faculty, grants and foundation support, and there is no reason for that to change. But as the economic future is more widely understood, continual competition in the academic library sector will be recognized as counterproductive. Access to information will measure library quality, not the number of titles owned.

2. *Accreditation Standards.* In the real world, collection size is an increasingly inappropriate standard of library excellence. Unfortunately, the accreditation agencies that control academic life are reactive and resistant to change. But they will have to change. Accrediting agencies will face strong pressure to amend the rules and recognize the emergence of new standards of library quality such as breadth of database, ease of accessibility, and speed of document delivery.

3. *Rewards.* A librarian gains few personal rewards in the short term for behaving cooperatively. There are no connected salary increases, bonuses, granting of tenure, or advancement in rank. In fact, cooperation begets risk. Cooperation implies contributing something of value to gain a collective advantage and carries with it some loss of control. This is an important issue, particularly within the library community with its history of aversion to risk.

4. *Commonality.* Consortia are many and diverse. Probably no two are alike. They were created to deal with specific issues and do not immediately provide an established framework upon which to develop the National Electronic Library. The task would be easier if these organizations were identical. The task also would be easier if these member organizations had a more positive performance record.

However, for reasons stated earlier, consortia are expected to commit themselves to the national agenda. That they are diverse and have a reputation for inaction are facts of life. But when the magnitude of the issue is broadly understood, it is the new common agenda that will define consortia, not their history.

5. *Library Schools.* Today, the library school curriculum is under close scrutiny. There are widespread negative perceptions among university administrators about library program viability. While library school survival is not a consortial issue per se, continued uncertainty about this issue could marginalize an important natural ally. It is important that library school faculty are able to give wide-spread, high-profile support to the benefits of resource sharing through consortial action.

THE CASE FOR CONSORTIA

Hawkins quotes Patricia Battin: "If the scholarly world is to maintain control of and access to its knowledge, both new and old, new cooperative ventures must be organized for the management of knowledge itself, rather than the ownership of formats" (Battin 1989: 382). Richard Dougherty tells us: "Participation in a library consortium may be described as an investment in broad-scale scholarly interaction that provides direct intellectual benefits. It constitutes an investment . . . in scholarly communication that no individual library and few universities could afford to support" (Dougherty 1988: 23). If only we could work together. We can. Hawkins's economic case is incontrovertible. He persuasively argues that the academic library will not scale into the next century using the current model. Funding will continue to fall further behind the exponentially increasing volume and cost of information, and even if somehow we found acquisition funds, we couldn't afford to construct the buildings to house the new material. He points us toward the electronic solution and challenges us to move quickly.

Of course, inadequate library funding is an old story. The problem has been with us for a long time. Only now are we beginning to recognize its seriousness. This belated recognition is due to librarians performing their jobs too well. Librarians have shielded us from the truth by careful trimming of acquisitions, internal budget transfers, strategic shifts in staffing, increased utilization of automated library systems and, regrettably, deterioration in service.

But the threshold has been crossed. We know that fresh ideas and resources are needed. A little help will be forthcoming even if we don't act. It will be possible to deliver some new money to librarians. After all, public administrators are becoming increasingly sensitive to the importance of widespread availability of information. And all the drum beating about the information highway will have some positive benefit. But the bottom line is that the competition for dollars is fierce, and there is no reason to believe that conditions will improve. Funding requests will need to look like business plans, couched in terms of return on investment.

In the past, we have pitched our library budget requests to the decision makers in terms of social, educational, and research value. To be candid, we also have not been above trading on the reverence that society feels toward libraries in general. Distinguished historian and television celebrity Shelby Foote has our message down pat. He has captured our feelings perfectly in his statement that ''a university is just a group of buildings gathered around a library. The library is the university'' (Foote 1994: 984).

But times have changed. Money is scarce and administrators need to be educated about our vision of the electronic library. The budget request strategies of the past, in which we argued for incremental fund increases to meet increased student and faculty demands adjusted for inflation, need to be rethought. There is a more persuasive message, one which addresses a more urgent institutional goal, and that is the goal of institutional survival. Those higher education administrators who understand that the issue of universal access to information will separate the winners from the losers in the next century will support the electronic library and, as a result, their institutions will prosper.

There is another source of funds. This source is within our control, but it takes a great deal of imagination and hard work to get to it. And that is the existing funding base. This resource will not be accessed through Hawkins's tithing scheme, but can be accessed through program efficiencies. Old methods can be retired and these funds made available for new initiatives. The crisis will force library administration to make the hard choices. Many of the cost-saving strategies are well known, outsourcing of cataloging being the current hot button. There are others, all turning on the idea that a stand-alone library is fundamentally inefficient and that the best alternative is collective action. Even the OCLC, established in the early 1970s, represents one of the best examples of collective action among libraries.

Not only will difficult economic conditions force libraries to think more collectively, but also, the relationship between libraries and publishers will change. The marketplace will demand it. Much of the present financial squeeze arises from relentless increases in the cost of serials. All the usual strategies have been employed to cope with the problem: internal budget transfers, canceling subscriptions, widespread resource sharing, and greater reliance on electronic journal sources such as UnCover. Librarians have done all they can. The publishing industry now will have to change.

Financial pressures are causing academic administrators to become increasingly vocal about what they see as paying twice for campus-sponsored work, once in the professor's paycheck and again through the library acquisition budget. Technology has presented a viable electronic alternative to printed journals. The library can be the publisher.

The idea is attractive, and not merely as a cost-saving strategy. There is no inherent reason why a library-centered electronic journal cannot be thoroughly professional and important. In certain fields of research where quick access to current work is important, the electronic journal is ideal.

The possible emergence of the library-publisher, along with changed campus rules about ownership of intellectual property, could well be the most significant outcome of the creation of the National Electronic Library. Libraries deciding to move in this direction undoubtedly will seek partners to provide breadth of material and to maintain high professional standards. Partnerships can be formed around academic disciplines, local and regional interests, or other consortial organizations.

As noted earlier, one of the strategies for dealing with increased journal costs has been to transfer funds from other library line items. In particular, books and monographs have suffered. Special collections which enrich and define the institution and its academic priorities have suffered. The result is duplicative collections. Basic core collections are repeated everywhere.

Resource sharing is the obvious answer to the problem—not resource sharing as it is currently practiced, slow and unresponsive, but resource sharing as it is now being discussed within the consortia of the country and as advocated by the Association of Research Libraries in its North American Interlibrary Loan and Document Delivery Project. The key features are electronic access and facilitated document delivery. The strength of the project lies in its ability to promote developments that will improve the delivery of library materials to users at costs that are sustainable for libraries.

Both the electronic journal idea and the electronically facilitated document delivery scheme are important changes that are based on partnerships. This is another example of favorable positioning, consortia being in the right place at the right time.

The consortium also offers an effective way for libraries to keep pace with changes in learning. A different kind of scholarship and education is emerging from the electronic library. Research can now be undertaken that up until a few years ago was impossible, and from locations far removed from the central library facility. Distance learning and lifelong learning now can become reality.

In a recent article, "The Age of Social Transformation," Peter F. Drucker states, "Knowledge workers will give the emerging knowledge society its character, its leadership, its social profile. They may not be the ruling class of the knowledge society, but they are already its leading class" (Drucker 1994: 64). He is talking about the same people that we are attempting to reach with the national electronic library and distance and lifelong learning.

Drucker states further that:

In the knowledge society, clearly, more and more knowledge and especially advanced knowledge, will be acquired well past the age of formal schooling and increasingly, perhaps, through educational processes that do not center on the traditional school. . . . Increasingly, an educated person will be somebody who has learned how to learn, and continues learning, especially by formal education, through his or her lifetime. (Drucker 1994: 66–67)

We know what we are looking for. The discussion is only about getting there and whether placing our faith in the library community, organized into a multiplicity of consortia, is warranted.

This chapter uses a very broad definition of consortia, ranging from organizations created and funded by state legislatures to those grown out of informal librarian get-togethers. In spite of such historical differences, consortia appear to follow a pattern. They have the following identifying characteristics:

1. commitment to an agreed-upon mission statement, usually narrow in scope;
2. extremely democratic operating style, using committees extensively, discussing issues at great length, and making decisions by consensus;
3. minimal formal organizational structure, except where the consortium was created by statute or is a nonprofit corporation;
4. organized within a state or region;
5. a membership willing to commit significant amounts of time and staff to consortial activities; and
6. frequent opportunities for professional interaction among peers.

This admittedly generous definition is intended to be as inclusive as possible. However, it does stop short of including the not-for-profit cataloging and reference utilities that have evolved from consortia but which now clearly operate in the corporate environment. OCLC, Research Libraries Information Network (RLIN), Western Library Network (WLN), and the University of Toronto Library Automation System (UTLAS) are not considered consortia for our purposes, but they obviously will play an ever more important role in electronic library development.

The National Electronic Library will be built upon a foundation of the hundreds of groups, associations, alliances, and partnerships which already are diligently and cooperatively working toward subsets of our common goal. They include the Colorado Alliance of Research Libraries of course, but also organizations like Ohiolink, Illinet, the Florida Cooperative Library Association, the Triangle Research Libraries Network, the California Division of Library Automation, Marmot, CW/Mars Inc., Libraries of Middlesex Automation Consortium, and The Library Consortium. These established consortia have solid credentials and enough energy and growth potential to take leadership roles in the push to the next level.

Furthermore, new organizations seem to be popping up everywhere. Is there a state in the union that has not recently held some sort of summit conference on the subject of the information highway? Although too often the motivation for these conferences is the political concern by the participants that the information highway will bypass their state, forever condemning them to second-class status, these conferences are important. The more the issue is discussed, the better.

There is a great deal of momentum building at the state level. Perhaps this is attributable to these summit conferences, but more likely it is attributable to the ever-increasing public awareness of the issue. Interesting state-level projects are being reported regularly in the professional periodicals.

The State of Maine has announced that it currently is repackaging its telecommunications network into a separate state institution and expanding its scope. The State of Virginia has begun developing what it sees as a "virtual library" through which students everywhere in the state could electronically gain access to library resources. As they get the message, state legislatures all across the country can be expected to jump at the cost-saving implications of these and similar initiatives. Minnesota and Florida are among the states that have already done so.

What follows now is the specific case for consortia. The previous discussion presented general background information and highlighted factors to be considered in forming strategies for achieving the National Electronic Library goal. It is this chapter's argument that consortia can best get the job done because:

1. *Consortia already exist.* There is no need to create a new structure. Consortia are in place or are being put in place all across the country. Admittedly they are not interconnected. At present they have separate and perhaps conflicting agendas, and they often suffer from nagging local issues. At worst consortia represent a foundation upon which to build, and at best, operating pieces of the national superstructure.

2. *They can provide bottom-up support.* Only consortia can deliver support from the entire library community. The tradition of consensus which might be considered a flaw in the academic library culture also is an advantage in this instance. Each voice is listened to, each idea is respectfully considered, and major policy decisions are made collectively. A powerful force is created when agreement is reached. This bottom-up feature is crucial. A top-down solution, no matter how elegant, has little likelihood of acceptance in this environment.

Of course there is the potential for "death by committee." There are many examples of good ideas that were destroyed by the process of detailed deliberation. The expectation in this case is that the National Electronic Library is different, an idea so important that it won't be subjected to "business as usual."

3. *Consortia can assist in neutralizing opposition.* Support for the National Electronic Library will not be unanimous. As egos and money get involved, negative attitudes will develop. The consortial structure can assist in neutralizing such opposition in two ways: (1) by peer pressure within the organization to support the shared vision, and (2) by providing an organized counterbalance to outside interests.

4. *Consortia own the concept.* Of course, consortia aren't the only owners. The vision of a National Electronic Library is widely shared and it is important that the ownership feeling spread as far as possible. But for reasons that are obvious, feelings about ownership of the National Electronic Library concept are a little stronger in the library community. The National Electronic Library

really is a librarian's vision. While it may have been created in general academic discourse and therefore widely endorsed, the vision is expressed in the language of librarians. The idea of universal access to all information in all media via one terminal belongs to the library community. The vision clearly calls for sharing of resources.

5. *Consortia can attract funding.* As previously suggested, library dollars are scarce and budget request strategies will need improvement. In this climate, consortia can provide good funding targets. Consortia can offer economies of scale and general efficiencies that individual institutions cannot match. State legislatures are often confused by competition among state schools and are at a loss about finding equity in the relationship between public and private institutions. An appropriation to a statewide consortium promises efficient and balanced use of state funds.

It is an easy step from a single-purpose statewide consortium to one undertaking a more comprehensive agenda. Positioning makes this possible. Issues such as outsourced cataloging, interlibrary loan, union catalogs, document delivery, shared database access, creation of local specialized databases, volume purchasing, and common standards of interconnectivity all can be best addressed collectively.

6. *Consortia are easy to establish.* There are no rules needed. Natural groupings form as common interests and problems are identified. The members can choose to be very formal as in the Colorado Alliance, a 501(c)(3) not-for-profit corporation registered in Colorado with lengthy articles of incorporation, organizational bylaws, and formal software agreements. Or an informal consortium can limit itself to a mission statement, meeting agendas, and meeting minutes.

7. *Consortia are flexible.* Consortia can be whatever size they need to be. Although the reaction time is often painfully slow, consortia can expand or contract as circumstances warrant. Consortia can often be faulted on the downside for failure to disband when the mission has been accomplished or the reason for being has disappeared. But they are excellent on the upside, energetically undertaking important new responsibilities. In addition, consortia have fewer purchasing and contract constraints than do many libraries which must operate under the guidelines of local and state governments.

CONCLUSION

The case for consortia is based on positioning. Consortia are in the right place at the right time. The organized library community owns the vision and, given the financial realities, is motivated to work cooperatively toward its implementation.

The viability of hundreds of colleges and universities is hanging in the balance. All desire to survive. Some won't, killed off by their inability to comprehend twenty-first-century arithmetic.

A national electronic *something* will happen. That is clear from the many forces at work. Unfortunately, the forces are pulling in more than one direction. If we desire to have a National Electronic Library as described in our vision statement, then we must recommit ourselves to resource sharing. The consortial structure appears to be the most promising way to get there.

REFERENCES

Battin, Patricia. 1989. "New Ways of Thinking About Financing Information Services." In *Organizing and Managing Resources on Campus*, ed. Brian L. Hawkins. McKinney, TX: Academic Computing Publications, p. 382.

Dougherty, Richard M. 1988. "Research Library Networks: Leveraging the Benefits." *Academe* (July/August): 22–25.

Drucker, Peter F. 1994. "The Age of Social Transformation." *The Atlantic Monthly* (November): 53–80.

Foote, Shelby. 1994. "Writers at Work: How Libraries Shape the Muse." *American Libraries* (December): 984.

Gibbs, W. Wayt. 1994. "Software's Chronic Crisis." *Scientific American* (September): 86–95.

Hawkins, Brian L. 1994. "Creating the Library of the Future: Incrementalism Won't Get Us There!" *Serials Librarian* 24, no. 3/4: 17–47.

Luskin, Bernard J. 1994. "Some Dreams and Realities for the Digital Highway." Dinner address, Denver, CO, September 25.

3

The Academic Institution and the National Electronic Library

Thomas M. Peischl

The rapid and rampant changes in the world of information have captured the attention of university and college administrators. There are approximately 3,600 such academic institutions of post-secondary education. Each has its own model library, each has its own vision of the future, and each has its own forces driving that future. It is axiomatic that two of the major forces driving all institutions are (1) the desire for a secure future and (2) attracting customers (students) who are willing to buy the services offered (an education).

It is no longer enough to speak of library resources; today it is necessary to speak of "information" and all it stands for. Library resources are a mere part of information resources. The university is awash with information; the university imports and exports information; the university creates and manipulates information; the university thrives on information; and the university would shrivel without information. The university, through its administrators, faculty, and staff, is looking to its professionals to bring semblance and control out of this condition. The library, the traditional organization responsible for information, has the unenviable task of bringing cohesion and sanity to an insane world of limitless, borderless, unharnessed, raw information.

The purpose of this chapter is to represent the university's view of the future of information and to discuss problems and opportunities as presented by various administrators external to the library. It is divided into five sections. Section one is a brief representation of the thoughts and concerns about the library and information by major university officers in the administrative, academic, financial, and student affairs areas. Section two highlights the challenges to higher education as seen by these officers. Section three outlines challenges to the library, and section four summarizes with a brief speculation of the confluence of various information services. The chapter ends with a list of readings for further consideration and thought.

THOUGHTS AND CONCERNS OF THE LIBRARY AND INFORMATION

The president of the university, as the chief executive officer, is in a unique position to be ultimately responsible for many activities and programs without the necessity of having a depth of knowledge about them. Yet the CEO, the symbol of university leadership, must be conversant with all aspects of the academy. Many presidents profess a yearning to be back in the classroom where teaching and learning are the important realities. The library was for them a pleasant, quiet place, filled with books and helpful professionals, where one went to read, study, and contemplate the deeper meaning of life. Today the library represents to these same presidents a high-cost service center where expenses are continually escalating at a rate greater than inflation and where the future is about as clear as mud.

Presidents favor the philosophy that faculty should be professional educators, not teachers of a discipline. As professional educators, they enhance the outcome-based nature of the educational activities of students of all ages. Being responsible for the content and delivery of learning, the faculty set their own professional standards and the standards for access to and delivery of information. The truth of the problem is that faculty are professional in their discipline and totally competent in their subject matter. However, no mechanism is in place to establish or encourage their competence as directors of the educational experiences of students, especially for the delivery of information resources in the brave new information world.

A weighty concern of presidents is accountability. Accountability, a most pernicious buzzword, requires that the appropriate information is used to make correct decisions which are defensible by other appropriate information! Those responsible for the funding of an institution of higher education, whether legislators, governing boards, parents, grant-funding corporations, and even the tuition-paying consumers themselves, demand the satisfaction that their funds are well invested. This requires increasingly more information to answer increasingly complex questions. The information professionals, in addition to their already overwhelming task of helping the academic customers, must assist the president in providing the appropriate information for accountability to those who require it.

The Higher Education Information Resource Alliance's Executives Strategies Report #2 (Cummings et al. 1992: 3–4) took a historical look at the problem of the library of the future and postulated seven transitional issues which presidents needed to consider in moving from a paper-based library organization to alternative types of scholarly communication. They are summarized here because they succinctly cover the broad transitional issues, but they do not specify how the library will operate after the transition.

First, because the act of publishing is so important in the traditional academic reward system, any change will have to replace the process of peer review to retain any credibility. Second, the mechanisms for the distribution of texts will change, and thus new algorithms will need to be certified which please the traditional and electronic publishers, consumers, and libraries as depositories. Third, the campus telecommunications infrastructures need vast upgrading, and attention must be paid to the tiered structure of national, regional, and local-area networks. Fourth, the national network must be defined and supported. Fifth, standards for retrieval protocols and digital representation of information must be established. Sixth, the traditional roles in the publishing process will change significantly. Universities must consider a larger role in the scholarly communication process. Finally, the current copyright legislation will not serve the new world of electronic publishing.

The traditional mission of the university library is to supply information resources in all formats, to provide professional interpretive services, and to provide a quiet study space to support the teaching, learning, and research missions of the University. Because of this important mission, the library, second only to the faculty, is near and dear to the vice-president for academic affairs, the provost, or whomever is the leader of the academic mission of the University.

The vice-president for academic affairs (VPAA), more than the president, is acutely aware of the spiraling costs of the traditional library paper resources, especially periodicals. They are quite familiar with charts such as Figure 3.1, which graphically illustrates what has been known for years; journals and other library materials have been rising in cost faster than other higher education goods and services.

Each VPAA has a favorite personal model for the past and current library which evolved from his or her particular set of needs and experiences while a professor. To some the library is a warehouse, a repository of books and a noninstructional center, costly but necessary for the academy. To others, the library supports direct reading assignments while storing other things just in case they are needed by some researcher. Still others see the library as an independent learning center, supplementing the activities of direct classroom instruction.

The most important recent change in the library has been the introduction of nontactile, Boolean search logic. The traditional method of searching for library materials is second nature to the typical professor. The computer not only prohibits the tactile sensations of shuffling through the card files, but it also forces dramatic behavioral changes that alter the very nature of the relationship between the searcher and the materials. Many a provost has spent hours and hours with professors mourning the loss of an era and, more importantly, the alleged

Figure 3.1
Comparing the CPI, HEPI, and USPPI

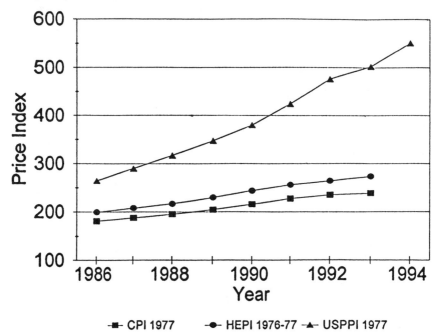

CPI = Consumer Price Index as reported by the U.S. Bureau of Labor Statistics. For the purposes
     of this study, the CPI was recalculated to a base year of 1977 in order to provide a common
     base for historical comparison. CPI numbers were converted to a base year of 1977 by mul-
     tiplying each index number by 100 then dividing by 181.5 (the CPI for 1977).
HEPI = Higher Education Price Index published by the Research Associates of Washington, *Higher
     Education Prices and Price Indexes: 1993 Update.*
USPPI = The U.S. Periodical Price Index measures the average annual subscription prices of U.S.
     periodicals and is the responsibility of the Library Materials Price Index Committee of the
     American Library Association.
The numbers are taken from Carpenter and Alexander (1994): 453.
Thanks to Joanna Mitchell, Northern Michigan University.

loss of information resulting from this new-fangled retrieval method. These same
VPAAs have spent a disproportionate amount of time on the nonconverts in
comparison to the converts who have been leading the way to new, improved,
and vastly more effective research storage and retrieval techniques.

True, many faculty aggressively push the envelope to the next level of use
and inspire other faculty and students. They are finding that vast amounts of
information are available but often inaccessible due to a lack of familiarity with
electronic networks. An initial lack of confidence with searching results, and the
initial requirement of spending an excessive amount of time on the process and
not the product, is giving way to satisfaction with self-searching and/or with

trusting information professionals to facilitate searching in a time-saving fashion.

What are the thoughts of the future of the library from the office of the provost? It is clear that they draw their models from the largest camp, the silent majority of faculty. The library will be a technology center with faculty as resource managers, not merely content providers. The battle will be between those who wish to teach subject content and those who wish to teach others to learn how to learn. Most universities are structured on the model of the research university—discipline by discipline. It may be that another model is more appropriate. Professors think they know their disciplines, but there is always someone in the wings who knows more. One can never know everything about a subject. Is it not conceivable that, beyond the rudiments, it is much better to teach learning techniques than subject content? Why cannot faculty development be seen as increasing the efficiencies of learning rather than only adding to the knowledge base of the discipline? It will be necessary to improve the efficiencies of higher education because both those directly paying tuition and those supporting tuition through the payment of taxes will not continue to support higher education at its current inflation rate. Someone will find a better, cheaper method of instructing and will improve the learning process, most likely through the use of technology. Faculty must become masters of the learning process, not just conveyors of knowledge. These changes will significantly dictate the library and information services of the future.

The primary concern of financial management professionals is slowing the escalation of the cost of an education. Higher education is big business. Public and private college and university expenditures exceeded $156 billion in 1991–1992, according to the National Center for Education Statistics (1994: 344). This amount of money was spent to educate slightly more than 7.5 percent of the population of the country. With public appropriations and other income remaining flat or declining, with intense competition for recruiting and retaining new students, and with the demand that tuition increases remain at or below the inflation rate, campus financial planners are struggling to retard the cost escalation.

Cost containment means either increasing income or cutting costs from current operations such as printing, telephone service, internally funded research, release time, public services, and institutional support. Fiscal administrators are assuming that revenues will remain flat and expenses will continue to rise. Two obvious solutions are to either drop some services and programs or to reallocate current resources within the university. Each university operation must undergo a self-analysis to look for efficiencies and to seek methods of improving the delivery of services. Services not contributing to the core mission of the university will need to be dropped to reduce unnecessary overhead. Personnel compensation constitutes approximately 70 percent of all university expenses. While it is humane and rational to begin looking for efficiencies with nonpersonnel operations, real savings will be possible only when personnel efficiencies are put on the agenda as well.

The library is an expensive cost center whose programs have been largely accepted on blind faith by university management because data for decision making have been scarce or nonexistent. The need for better data has never been more obvious. Technology has not lowered the cost of information services, nor has investment in technology equated to lower costs in the library's programs. The pay-back may be in improved quality of service to the users, but librarians must be able to verify that to the campus administrators. Information resources need not reside locally, and librarians should quickly determine alternative, cost-effective methods of delivering services before it is done for them by the for-profit sector. Fewer items are being purchased, and though new services are being initiated, library customers are becoming disenchanted with the ability of the library to provide the necessary information resources. Libraries have been labor intensive and it appears that they will remain so. Rather than eliminating the need for librarians or information professionals, current technology requires better-trained professionals if users are to be properly served. The explosion of information resources without commonly accepted standards, the introduction of electronic connectivity, and the concomitant demands from Generation X for better and quicker delivery dictate that libraries plan to change their modus operandi or implode from the weight of their services.

Financial professionals do not understand the complexity of the problems but they have the solution. Library business as usual must cease, and compelling evidence must be presented which assures the university that expenditures for information are being spent in the best manner possible to enhance the institutional mission.

Institutional Research (IR) professionals are intrigued by the new library because of all the data that are becoming available electronically. The old, traditional library was a great warehouse of data, unattainable except by the masochistic few with time on their hands and a need to bury their heads in dusty books. IR professionals need data the way other humans need air. The library of the future promises vast amounts of data from anywhere in the world which can be vacuumed up and massaged into meaningful statistics. This promise of nirvana has the IR folks ecstatic because finally there are data available to answer every problem and provide guidance for university planning. Decision makers find data habit forming—the more data there are, the more are needed to make better decisions. The information professionals among librarians may well be the ones who assist in keeping this habit in check by understanding and interpreting data to customers. If this occurs, the institutional research professionals will move into analysis and analytical studies and allow the library professionals to move into the areas of availability and interpretation. Librarians will become true information professionals by moving into the areas of administrative and forecasting data. These data do not belong to the library; often they are not even in the library. At present the library provides the electronic gateway to the sources. This will not be the case forever. The IR professionals are just scraping the surface of this new process of finding and exploiting data. What will happen to the library when this phenomenon becomes *de rigueur* and the entire university understands the process? Databases are being miniaturized on compact discs (CDs) and appearing faster than they can be understood. Massive databases are being produced cheaply, and organizations are selling back to universities data gathered from them. Databases are useful only if their information can explain phenomena and answer questions. What will the library professional be doing about this?

Finally, IR professionals feel that data for meaningful decisions about the library of the future and its information programs are not very useful. Although libraries have been gathering data forever, these data do not automatically lead to decisions made with confidence. Other academic areas of the university use benchmarking data to measure current service levels and to project future service levels. Student credit hours per faculty is one such example which aids managers in personnel decisions. The library is shy or devoid of such data, and what data exist seem to have little use for IR planning. For example, what does it mean that x million individuals exited the library during some measured time? What does it mean that x million current periodicals were removed from the shelves in a given time? And finally, what is the significance of having the book stock numbers published regularly? The new library must eliminate such useless quantitative data and must search for qualitative indicators that are relevant to the mission of the university.

The information technology (IT) professionals feel that we are all slow learners in higher education. History repeats itself because we do not learn from it! What goes around comes around. These and other trite, but sometimes true, sayings are applicable to the information technology revolution that is the latest movement to save the university.

Approximately two decades ago media technology was poised to save students from dreary, ineffective lectures which were the bane of undergraduate life. The "new" information technology is again poised to save students from the same dreary, boring lectures by some of the same professors! This time the fix must work for three reasons: First, the universities are going broke paying the high salaries of a soon-to-be-retired generation of pre-media professors; second, this generation of undergraduates, Generation X or Generation 13, grew up on MTV and computer games and must be educated through "edutainment," and third, it has been reported that this generation reads only under severe duress.

Information technology organizations vary with the personality of the university and may include any and all of the following components: computer technology for both direct administrative support and direct and indirect instructional support, instructional development for classroom and presentation support, information processing support (broadly defined to include the traditional and the evolving electronic library), distance education programming and technology support, printing, duplication and publication (often included with the new book store concept), public radio, and public television. Instructional technology is a more dated nomenclature for a subset of these services which emphasized technology for use in the classroom to supplement the traditional lecture method. The modern IT is meant to support a broader, all inclusive, packaging of subject content including the information resources, the information sources, and the process of delivering subject content in various formats designed for specific learning styles.

The traditional library plays only a minor role in this new IT process and can be circumvented most of the time. What attracts IT professionals to the library is threefold: (1) Librarians, as information specialists, know where information resides, how to retrieve it, and how to exploit it; (2) librarians know how to speak and work with faculty, students, and other information users; and (3) perhaps most important, the library has the biggest physical space available on campus which can be remodeled for other purposes. If the future of information is digital, the university need only to digitize the paper collections and purchase the scholars and production workstations! The traditional library will be transformed into an information arcade, an information kiosk, or an information center as many are already titled.

It is not a question of whether this change is coming. The question is what part will the traditional library and current and future librarians play in the transformation of the teaching-learning process on campus. Librarians may have been the first information specialists, but the technology driving the information revolution is causing great changes in the library and on the campus. Are librarians prepared for this and will librarians assist the information technology professionals in making the necessary changes to the campus culture?

These are difficult times for student affairs professionals. In addition to fighting for their very survival on some campuses, they are expected to understand and generate programming for Generation 13, for the increasing proportion of reentering or nontraditional students, and for the extremely diverse populations now entering college. At the same time they are tasked with helping current and new faculty initiate the necessary changes in the delivery of education in order to succeed with the traditional audiences as well as with the new customers.

Student affairs professionals do not know how to react at times so they imitate academic affairs professionals. This mistake is at the very core of the problem. While it begs other more relevant questions, it does go a long way toward explaining why the instructional faculty are mostly complacent about student affairs programs and why student affairs efforts to unify the undergraduate experience into a total maturation schema rather than a separate academic and a personal growth schema are failing.

Student affairs professionals note the fact that today's students, mostly Generation X, are in the "quick and dirty" phase of their lives. They want education and jobs with minimal involvement of time and energy and even less commitment. Astin's plea (1993: 365) that "time on task" is correlated with quality and commitment is not relevant to this generation of students. Ease of access and ease of accomplishment is more important than working long and hard for success.

Some universities have model programs which span the academic/personal growth continuum. The programs are meant to blend and to provide the student with the tools for learning and growing in an environment of comfort and understanding. The environment must be supporting, allowing for trial, error, and readjustment without toxic failure and without deflating the self-worth of the individual. Some major initiatives in this area are freshman year experience programs, live-in academic advisors, and having faculty available to social clubs and groups for academic and personal advising. The library, although being usually aligned with the academic side of the university, is also responsible for programming a supportive environment where students may be active or passive, where students may learn by trial and error without fear of failure, and where students are accepted anywhere along the academic/personal growth continuum.

CHALLENGES TO HIGHER EDUCATION
AS SEEN BY ADMINISTRATORS

Higher education systems as well as individual universities are facing more challenges than at any other time in history. While this is true, unfortunately successful answers to past challenges are not guides or solutions to the current challenges. New thinking, new frameworks, and new problem solving strategies are required. This section lists some of the significant challenges to the university as seen by administrators.

The politics of higher education is the primary challenge to administrators. Despite data to the contrary, the implied importance of higher education as an asset in filling the need for trained and educated citizens and workers has diminished in the past decade. Legislators in the United States allocate over $40 billion in direct support to higher education and they cannot determine what they are getting for their money. The output or product of colleges and universities, be it training, education, or the creation of new knowledge, is difficult to quantify in acceptable terms to external observers. It is in vogue to speak of customers, who are always right. Yet colleges and universities serve such disparate customers that being "right" in today's society requires significant, speedy, internal changes which have been unacceptable heretofore in the academy. And being right today does not guarantee correctness tomorrow.

Productivity is a challenge related to the politics of higher education. The definition of productivity in the academy is unclear and difficult to measure. Faculty are adverse to defining productivity beyond the technical data accumulated electronically indicating student credit hours generated per faculty and other data of that nature. Future teaching will require that many more students are mentored, not directly taught, by fewer faculty. Productivity in the creation of new knowledge must also undergo revision. New definitions of productivity and increasing that productivity, however defined, will benefit public relations with those responsible for funding higher education.

The changing workforce is a third important challenge to the stability and future of higher education. By the end of this century close to 60 percent of the current faculty will retire. This aging, predominantly white male work force is making room for a more diverse cohort who do not have the same institutional history, and who do not relate to the values held by the current faculty. The enculturation of the coming generation of faculty is too critical to be the sole responsibility of the current faculty. The challenge for administrators (who incidentally emerged from this current workforce) is to respect and honor the current generation of faculty for their contributions while working with young faculty to develop new expectations, new productivity standards, and a new culture of higher education.

Diversity is a challenge in all areas of society today. Higher education, a microcosm of the larger world, is equally challenged by diversity. The culture of higher education changes slowly while the expectations of those seeking education are geared to speedy changes. The demographics clearly show a maturing population that is considerably different from past generations. Generation 13 and younger students are nothing like those who proceeded them through college. The challenge is to program for these differences in meaningful ways, to celebrate these differences while honoring the past, and to ensure equity of advantages for all regardless of socioeconomic status, gender, or ethnicity. This is no small task, given the slow pace of change in higher education bureaucracies.

The challenge of diversity might be more easily resolved if universities did not assume the righteousness of their mission, another challenge as seen by insiders. Universities are in the business of changing lives without really completely understanding what is important to the students. The university assumes it knows what is right. There is a necessity to inquire of the students what broad continuous support is needed in and out of the classroom while assuming some responsibility for guiding students through this search. This generation demands and requires more input into the process than prior generations. The righteousness of mission is blocking the acceptance of students as true partners in this relationship. The students need a support continuum where classroom instruction is only one point. Other support services, including the library, must be offered, and all university professionals must be more in tune to the needs of individual students along this continuum. University policies generally allow students the opportunity to be active or passive and to make their own decisions. This forces students to live with their personal decisions. While such independence is appropriate for some students, others need periodic direct intervention and help. The university experience must be more of a partnership, a collaborative adventure between student and mentor designed to produce a citizen who makes decisions based on acceptable norms.

Paralysis by analysis is another challenge for higher education. ''A parked car cannot be steered'' is a saying indicating the slowness of change in higher education. Ideally, universities are in the business of introducing change, of teaching about change, and of initiating change. But change occurs slowly within academic departments, colleges, and universities. Tom Peters (1983: 119 ff) wrote that a bias for action is one sign of a healthy organization. Many universities do not fall into this category. Universities must begin to look for efficiencies in every way they do business, beginning in the classroom right up to the board room. Business as usual will not do in the future. The academic reward system, based on the publish or perish model, must change. Being a good teacher is not good enough either. Alternative measurements of efficiency and quality must arise from within, or external agencies will impose standards and programs without consultation.

The age of technology has arrived at the university. The growing demand for all kinds of technology is driving most budgeting processes. Technology is driving educational philosophy and practice rather than the other way around. If we cannot measure the impact of technology, and we cannot at the moment, it is difficult to measure appropriate efficiencies in technology which support education. Dougherty and Hughes reported in *Preferred Futures for Libraries* (1991: 14) that administrators focused solely on the trends of technology cost and make decisions based on that criterion when brainstorming about the future of higher education. That fact should surprise no one who works with budgets. The challenge to administrators is to accomplish appropriate missions by exploiting technology and budgets.

Another significant challenge to higher education is to overcome time and distance borders while maintaining quality standards. The traditional educational pipeline is too narrow for the new delivery systems. The current system, paper-based and geographically grounded, must give way to a broadbanded, timeless delivery system with no borders. New delivery methods are possible. First, appropriate technology is available although expensive. Second, the communication backbone, whether fiber, satellite, or open air broadcast, is available and in use commercially. Third, the customer base is growing as more nontraditional and/or place-bound consumers voice their requirements. Finally, senior faculty are retiring and being replaced by others who know the technology and who understand the need to engage in time-shifting, distance-neutral educational endeavors.

The final challenge according to higher education professionals is revamping the bureaucratic structure of higher education, from the statewide oversight systems down to the academic departments on individual campuses. The bureaucratic structures of statewide systems were created years ago when physical centralization was equated with accountability. Today, technology and market forces are negating the need for personnel-intensive central administrations that impede change even more than the campus bureaucracies find tolerable. Modern electronic post-audit techniques, along with the public's demand for smaller government, are making individual universities entrepreneurial public agencies. The single academic department is an arcane structure which has lost its relevance in modern higher education. Knowledge is cumulative and becomes of value only when the student is capable of synthesizing it with other subjects. In the past, academic departments emerged to promote the discipline and to bring semblance to the politics of education, not to promote cumulative and integrated learning. New models of teaching demand team mentoring across the traditional disciplines to educate individuals capable of succeeding in the future. The teacher who can lead the learning process as well as understand the rudiments of subject content will emerge as the successful teacher of tomorrow.

CHALLENGES TO THE TRADITIONAL LIBRARY AS SEEN BY ADMINISTRATORS

Many years ago Tom Galvin (1978), a former American Library Association (ALA) executive director, said in an informal presentation that librarians "need to know when enough is enough" in defending budgets and seeking resources. Librarians have never been able to indicate to management how much is enough, but they always have been able to report that more funds are needed for the purchase of resources. University administrators have been told that the cost of library materials has risen faster than inflation for many years. A recent ARL study funded by the Mellon Foundation (Cummings et al. 1992) determined that, contrary to conventional wisdom, library budgets have tended to increase less rapidly than other university expenditures. This study also found that the budgets for libraries studied have declined through the last decade to the point that they have lost almost all the ground gained in the preceding twenty years. Figure 3.1 clearly shows that material costs have and will continue to be a significant problem to all libraries. The challenge is obvious—to study and implement better, cost-effective ways to organize the traditional library to insure that professional services and appropriate information resources remain available for the future users whose use of time, distance and information will be significantly different from that of prior students.

The second enormous challenge for libraries is to bring closure to the problem of intellectual property rights, or copyright as it is known in the publishing arena. Many universities give up intellectual rights to commercial publishers and then proceed to buy them back in the form of publications. The Association of American Universities Research Libraries formed a task force and "charged [it] with developing proposals for university policies governing intellectual property ownership and rights in an electronic environment." This task proved daunting, as reported by ARL in May 1994. The task force could only recommend that "the Association of American Universities, working in partnership with the Association of Research Libraries, continue the process begun in this project." (Association of Research Libraries 1994: 107). The fact that the task force did not meet its charge only validates that intellectual property rights are a complex issue and will remain a major barrier to the resolution of the warehouse versus access conundrum.

A subset of the property rights question is the challenge of caring for the rotting paper-based inventories in university libraries. The problem is daunting. First, the present paper collections are deteriorating faster than library archivists or conservationists can rescue them. Second, saving the written text, especially primary writings, through micro format or digital technology, is unsuitable to many researchers. Third, there remains the question of intellectual property rights. Fourth, the copying equipment and personnel costs are excessively expensive. And finally, building or remodeling existing storage facilities with the appropriate humidity and temperature controls for delicate materials exceeds twenty dollars a volume. This conservation problem is being largely ignored because the solutions are too expensive and because other problems appear more pressing. In the meantime, valuable paper-based collections silently deteriorate.

There are administrators who are optimistic enough to suggest that the future of the library is as an instructional center, not a warehouse. The classroom instructor is responsible for the content learning of students. However, who is responsible for preparing undergraduates as life-long learners? Who is responsible for preparing them to search, find, and exploit information in the resolution of daily problems? Is it here that the information professionals will make their mark? Librarians have a chance to become active managers of information on campus, including the electronic systems which will be reallocated from existing resources and shifted to the organization which is capable of exploiting them in the most economic, efficient manner. When the library becomes an independent learning center coalescing the core support of the academic enterprise it will be seen as part of the solution, not part of the problem.

SUMMARY

The purpose of this chapter is to present university problems and opportunities as seen by various administrators. This chapter is not intended to answer the questions raised by the administrators but to provide the reader with the thoughts of administrative colleagues in the academy. The reader should by now understand that universities are not concentrating on the problem of the National Electronic Library, despite Hawkins's (1994b) passion for the issue. They are concentrating on the future of information services across the university, with the library being a part of the problem and resolution. It is up to librarians to determine what role they will play and what impact they will have on the future of these services. The administrative views and challenges recorded in this chapter should be daunting enough to keep librarians busy for the next decade, during which 60 percent of us will also retire. During this brief time librarians need to continue to champion the information technology revolution, the convergence of traditional library services and digital technology, for the information users of the next century.

SELECTED BIBLIOGRAPHY

Association of Research Libraries. 1994. *Reports of the AAU Task Forces on Intellectual Property Rights in an Electronic Environment.* Washington, DC: Association of Research Libraries.

Astin, Alexander. 1993. *What Matters in Colleges?* San Francisco: Jossey-Bass.

Atkins, Stephen E. 1991. *The Academic Library in the American University.* Chicago: American Library Association.

Bailey, C. W. 1993. "Public Access Computer Systems." *Information Technology and Libraries* 12: 99–106.

Baird, Marcia, and Mavis Monson. 1992. "Distance Education: Meeting Diverse Learners' Needs in a Changing World." *Distance Education* 51: 65–75.

Barone, Carole A. 1989. "Planning and the Changing Role of the CIO in Higher Education." *Information Management Review* 5: 23–31.

Becker, William E., and Darrell R. Lewis, eds. 1992. *The Economics of Higher Education.* Boston: Kluwer Academic Publishers.

Blegen, John. 1993. "Virtual Libraries, Real Cooperation: A View of the Coalition for Networked Information." *Illinois Libraries* 75: 247–250.

Brindley, Lynne, ed. 1989. *The Electronic Campus: An Information Strategy.* Cambridge, England: Cambridge University Press.

Butler, Brett. 1992. "Electronic Editions of Serials: The Virtual Library Model." *Serials Review* 18: 102–106.

Callan, Patrick M. 1986. *Environmental Scanning for Strategic Leadership.* San Francisco: Jossey-Bass.

Carpenter, K. Hammell, and A. W. Alexander. 1994. "U.S. Periodical Price Index for 1994." *American Libraries* 25, no. 5 (May): 453.

Carter, Richard B., Sree Nilakanta, and Daniel Norris. 1991. "Strategic Planning for Information Systems: The Evidence from a Successful Implementation in an Academic Setting." *Journal on Computing Research in Education* 24: 280–288.

Chronicle of Higher Education. 1994. *The Almanac.* Washington, DC.

Copyright Policy Task Force of the Triangle Research Libraries Network. 1993. *Model University Policy Regarding Faculty Publication in Scientific and Technical Journals.* Chapel Hill: Sunsite.unc.edu.

Corbin, Roberta A. 1991. "Development of the National Research Education Network." *Information Technology and Libraries* 10: 212–220.

Cummings, Anthony M. et al. 1992. *What Presidents Need to Know about the Future of University Libraries: Technology and Scholarly Communication.* Washington, DC: Association of Research Libraries.

Dougherty, Richard M., and Carol Hughes. 1991. *Preferred Futures for Libraries: A Summary of Six Workshops with University Provosts and Library Directors.* Mountain View, CA: Research Library Group.

Dougherty, Richard M., and Carol Hughes. 1993. *Preferred Library Futures II: Charting the Paths.* Mountain View, CA: Research Library Group.

Drabenstott, Karen M. 1993. *Analytical Review of the Library of the Future.* Washington, DC: Council on Library Resources.

Fox, Edward A. et al. 1991. "Users, User Interfaces, and Objects: Envision, a Digital Library." *Journal of the American Society for Information Science* 44: 480–491.

Fradkin, Bernard, and W. Lee Hisel. 1993. "Harnessing the Future: Administrative Support for Learning Resources." *Community College Journal* 63: 24–29.

Frank, Allan R., and Schuyler R. Lesher. 1991. "Planning for Executive Information Systems in Higher Education." *Cause/Effect* 14: 31–39.

Galvin, Tom. "Librarians and Campus Leadership." Informal talk given at the University of Northern Colorado, 1978. Not recorded or published.

Garrett, John. 1993. "Digital Libraries: The Grand Challenges." *Educom Review* 28: 17–21.

Guskin, Alan. 1994a. "Reducing Student Costs and Enhancing Student Learning. Part I." *Change* 26: 23–29.

Guskin, Alan. 1994b. "Reducing Student Costs and Enhancing Student Learning. Part II." *Change* 26: 16–25.

Handy, Charles B. 1989. *The Age of Unreason.* Boston: Harvard University Press.

Handy, Charles B. 1993. *Understanding Organizations.* New York: Oxford University Press.

Hawkins, Brian L. 1994a. "Creating the Library of the Future: Incrementalism Won't Get Us There!" *Serials Librarian* 24, no. 3/4: 17–47.

Hawkins, Brian L. 1994b. "Planning for the National Electronic Library." *Educom Review* 29: 19–29.

Heath, Fred M. 1993. "The Emerging National Information Infrastructure: An Interview with Paul Evan Peters and Jim Neal." *Library Administration and Management* 7: 200–207.

Heterick, Robert C. 1991. "Academic Sacred Cows and Exponential Growth." *Cause/Effect* 14: 9–14.

Hirshon, Arnold, ed. 1993. *After the Electronic Revolution, Will You Be the First to Go?* Chicago: American Library Association.

Jensen, Robert E. 1993. "The Technology of the Future Is Already Here." *Academe* 79: 8–13.

Kane, John D., and Sharon K. B. Wright. 1993. "A National Electronic Library for Youth Development." *Journal of Agricultural and Food Information* 1: 3–19.

King, Hanna. 1993. "Walls Around the Electronic Library." *Electronic Library* 11: 165–174.

Lancaster, F. W. 1993. *Libraries and the Future: Essays on the Library in the Twenty–First Century.* New York: Haworth Press.

Louis, Kenneth R. R. Gross. 1991. "The Real Costs and Financial Challenges of Library Networking: Part I." In *Networks, Open Access and Virtual Libraries: Implications for the Research Library.* Urbana-Champaign: University of Illinois Press, pp. 118–131.

Lyle, Guy R. 1963. *The President, the Professor and the College Library.* New York: H. W. Wilson.

Lynch, Clifford A. 1991. "The Development of Electronic Publishing and Digital Library Collections on the NREN." *Electronic Networking* 1: 6–22.

Malinconico, S. Michael. 1991. "Technology and the Academic Workplace." *Library Administration and Management* (Winter): 25–28.

Massy, William F. 1989. *A Strategy for Productivity Improvement in College and University Academic Departments.* Palo Alto, CA: Stanford Institute for Higher Education Research.

McClure, Charles 1992. "The High Performance Computing Act of 1991: Moving Forward." *Electronic Networking* 2: 2–10.

McClure, Charles R. et al. 1993. "Toward a Virtual Library: Internet and the National Research and Education Network." In *The Bowker Annual.* New Providence, NJ: R. R. Bowker, pp. 25–45.

McClure, Polly Ann, and James G. Williams. 1992. "Metamorphosis in Computing Services at Indiana University." *Cause/Effect* 15: 15–25.

McMahon, Suzanne et al., eds. 1992. *If We Build It: Scholarly Communications and*

Networking Technologies: Proceedings of the North American Serials Interest Group, Inc. New York: Haworth Press.

Miller, R. Bruce, and Milton T. Wolf. 1992. *Thinking Robots, An Aware Internet, and Cyberpunk Librarians.* Chicago: American Library Association.

Minter, John. 1994. *Management Ratios #8, Statistical Norms for College and Universities.* Boulder, CO: John Minter Associates.

Moore, Michael G. 1993. "Is Teaching Like Flying? A Total Systems View of Distance Education." *The American Journal of Distance Education* 7: 1–10.

National Center for Education Statistics. 1994. *Digest of Education Statistics, 1994.* Washington, DC: U.S. Department of Education.

OCLC. 1987. *Campus of the Future: Conference on Information Resources.* Dublin, OH: OCLC.

Peters, Thomas. 1983. *In Search of Excellence.* New York: Warner Books.

Saunders, Laverna M., ed. 1993. *The Virtual Library: Visions and Realities.* New York: Meckler Publishing.

Schatz, Bruce R. 1994. "Electronic Libraries and Electronic Librarians: Who Does What in a National Electronic Community." In *Emerging Communities: Integrating Networked Information into Library Services,* ed. Ann P. Bishop. Urbana-Champaign: University of Illinois.

Seiler, Lauren H. 1992. "The Concept of the Book in the Age of the Digital Electronic Medium." *Library Software Review* (January/February): 19–29.

Shaughnessy, Thomas W. 1992. "Approaches to Developing Competencies in Research Libraries." *Library Trends* 41: 282–298.

Shirato, Linda, ed. 1992, *Working with Faculty in the New Electronic Library.* Ann Arbor, MI: Pierian Press.

Sprague, Mary W. 1994. "Information-Seeking Patterns of University Administrators and Nonfaculty Professional Staff Members." *Journal of Academic Librarianship* 19: 378–383.

Twigg, Carol A. 1994. "The Need for a National Learning Infrastructure." *Educom Review* 29: 17–25.

Van Houwelin, Douglas E., and Michael J. McGill. 1993. *The Evolving National Information Network: Background and Challenges.* Washington, DC: The Commissions of Preservation and Access.

Ward, David. 1994. "Technology and the Changing Boundaries of Higher Education." *Educom Review* 29: 23–27.

Young, Peter R., and Jane Williams. 1994. "Libraries and the National Information Infrastructure." In *The Bowker Annual.* New Providence, NJ: R. R. Bowker, pp. 33–49.

4

The Public Enterprise and the National Electronic Library

Agnes M. Griffen

INTRODUCTION

"Twenty years from now," says Charlie Robinson, director of the Baltimore County Public Library, "there'll be no such thing as a library" (Jackson 1995: 49). Inspired by a vision of direct access to information primarily mediated through commercial vendors, he has already closed nine branch libraries and has installed a debit card system that provides the library with the capability of charging for every service. "People just don't give a rat's ass about free access to information," Robinson says (Jackson 1995: 50).

At the same time, across the country in San Francisco, Ken Dowlin is building a new large central library that will contain more than 800 work stations and is planned to be the hub of a community network that will connect to every home by the year 2000 (1993: 31–33). His vision of a

"Neographic Library . . . " is designed to deal with all formats of information, knowledge, and reading materials. . . . It will focus on connectivity with delivery to the user of all applicable formats, provide a Meta Catalog to the information and knowledge resources of the entire community, focus on access to the information and knowledge needed and used by the community it serves, and use current technology to manage resources and increase access. [It] is librarian-designed, but is access-oriented and user driven. The mission of the Neographic Library is the elimination of ignorance. (1993: 41)

In a six-year strategic plan for libraries in my own county, developed over the past year with extensive input from staff and citizens, we share a vision that, by 2001, public libraries will be "the gateway for easy and equitable access to information, ideas, and enrichment; where the lifelong learning needs of people will be met by a diverse staff through traditional services and new methods of information delivery" (Montgomery County, MD, Department of Public Libraries 1995: 1). The plan reaffirms a continuing need for library buildings filled with books and connected to computer networks.

Meanwhile, Montgomery County has completed renovation of almost all eleven older libraries and is selecting a site for a new community library to open in 1998, joining the six new libraries that have been built over the past fourteen years. At the same time, we continue to improve information services available through the CARL System, the prototype "National Electronic Library" to which we already are linked. We offer public access catalogs in all the libraries and local dial access to CARL as well as to SAILOR, Maryland's new statewide library network that connects citizens to the resources of all major libraries in the State and also serves as a gateway to the Internet. Recognizing the need for basic free access to the Internet, my staff and I also have been active participants over the past two years in developing CapAccess, the civic computing network for the Washington Metropolitan region.

So what is going on here? Even though our values and assumptions about access to information may be different, these varied responses reflect the awareness of public librarians that our contribution to the national public enterprise is the establishment at the local public library level of access points to the national information infrastructure that already is growing both spontaneously and by design. We are effectively building the public "on-ramps" to the information superhighway.

Many public librarians share with our academic colleagues the "very clear common vision of the future" that Brian L. Hawkins describes in his paper on "Planning for the National Electronic Library": that is, the concept of "universal access to information in all possible media via a single, multifunctional workstation" (1994: 20). To achieve the vision of universal access for all citizens, we must commit to principles that will ensure the public interest is met through the national information system to which this workstation will be connected.

Seven public interest principles were articulated last year by the Telecommunications Policy Roundtable (1994), a new coalition of 100 nonprofit and public interest organizations including national professional associations and educational institutions. Also in 1994, the American Library Association (ALA) published a similar document focused on key library concerns, "Principles for the Development of the National Information Infrastructure."

From the perspective of a public librarian who believes that the public interest will still be served in 2020 through public libraries, I will discuss four of these public interest principles that I believe are most critical to the health of the National Electronic Library. I will then identify four specific tasks or responsibilities that, in the spirit of these principles, public librarians are uniquely positioned to carry out in order to ensure that a National Electronic Library becomes a key component of the national information infrastructure, not only providing a major source of "content" but also serving all of the people, not just a select few.

THE PRINCIPLES WE SHARE

The seven principles promoted by the Telecommunications Policy Roundtable were intended to "reflect the values of a democratic government—openness, participation, and discussion." They were designed to influence public policy so that "new communications technologies [will] serve the democratic and social needs of our country" (1994: 2). These principles include:

1. *Universal Access*. All people should have affordable access to the information infrastructure.
2. *Freedom to Communicate*. The information infrastructure should enable all people to effectively exercise their fundamental right to communicate.
3. *Vital Civic Sector*. The information infrastructure must have a vital civic sector at its core.
4. *Diverse and Competitive Marketplace*. The information infrastructure should ensure competition among ideas and information providers.
5. *Equitable Workplace*. New technologies should be used to enhance the quality of work and to promote equity in the workplace.
6. *Privacy*. Privacy should be carefully protected and extended.
7. *Democratic Policy Making*. The public should be fully involved in policy making for the information infrastructure. (1994: 2–3)

I will comment briefly on the principles of universal access, freedom to communicate, vital civic sector, and privacy, demonstrating how critical they are to the development of the electronic library.

The first principle is "Universal Access. All people should have affordable access to the information infrastructure." "Making it possible for people to get information is the core mission of the profession of librarianship," says Jerry Campbell (1993: 560). Championing free and equal access for all people to the human record remains the basic mission of the public library and for all types of libraries that strive to serve all members of their constituency. W. David Penniman notes that "The information industry has said its vision is to provide information anywhere, anytime. Librarians must pursue a broader vision and assure a third component—for anyone" (1993: 19).

Public librarians have always focused on service for the individual, designing outreach programs for specific groups to open up access and extend the customer base to previously unserved individuals. In the constrained economic climate in which most tax-supported libraries must operate today, staffing is stretched thin and resources are scarce. To reduce employee workload and still keep up with growing demand, library managers are looking for ways to empower individual users to help themselves. Self-service checkout stations and other self-service functions such as automated telephone renewal, patron-placed holds and overdue notices, graphic user interfaces, user-friendly search strategies, and interactive directories are just some of the devices that libraries are beginning to use to reduce customer dependence on library staff. Looking even farther ahead, Dowlin envisions his multilingual Meta Catalog as "user-adaptive, sensing the skill level of the user and responding in appropriate languages or terminology" (Dowlin: 39). Surely what librarians are learning now as they improve self-service—both in-library and online—will make the national electronic library more easily accessible to everyone.

Public libraries and civic networks alike continue to struggle with the fact that fees are a major barrier to achieving universal access. "Affordable access" could mean different prices for people with different levels of income, but who is ready for a means test for public library cardholders? The policy statement notes that "Information that is essential in order to fully participate in a democratic society should be provided free" (1994: 2). This is why most public libraries provide a full range of basic services without a direct charge to the user. Lacking the time to engage in a full debate here on all aspects of "fee or free," I just want to note that as the focus shifts from ownership to access, the availability of electronic formats is putting these principles to a test in public libraries, with quite different responses in different settings. For example, some libraries that oppose fees unconditionally have refused to provide access at all to a fee-based document delivery service such as UnCover, even though the exchange of money is directly between the customer and the company, and its function as a basic index is provided without charge. Some have avoided fees by keeping costs down through rationing, metering, or limiting access through librarian mediation, while other libraries have developed policies that distinguish between basic free services and enhanced fee-based services.

Most public libraries that are committed to keeping services as free as possible are adopting what Hawkins recommends as funding mechanisms for the National Electronic Library in his nonprofit corporation model. Based on the Jeffersonian principle "that there should be free access," he suggests institutional, not user, payment for access, even to the extent that the National Electronic Library should "work with publishers to develop models for national and international site licenses . . . in the form of a contract allowing all citizens of a nation, or everyone without exception, access to the information in question" (1994: 23–27). Many libraries already do this for their own constituents and are looking at shared licenses as a function of the emerging statewide library networks. In Colorado, databases mounted on one site at one library are licensed to be available to all state residents; this is paid for jointly by participating libraries and/or with state funding. In an ultimate test of resource sharing, Hawkins also suggests "tithing" a portion of each library's materials budget to be set aside "to buy the rights to build [a shared] electronic library collection" (1994: 26).

A second basic principle is "Freedom to Communicate. The information infrastructure should enable all people to effectively exercise their fundamental right to communicate." While this principle is focused on protecting freedom of speech and preserving the free flow of information protected by the First Amendment, the idea of "guaranteeing the right of every person to communicate easily, affordably, and effectively" (1994: 2) in the telecommunications era has fascinating implications for the design of two-way library systems that offer self-service functions and libraries or civic computing networks that offer electronic mail.

In its seminal paper on "A National Strategy for Civic Networking: A Vision of Change," the Center for Civic Networking suggests that since "electronic mail over the public Internet effectively incurs no marginal cost . . . it should be provided as a public good to underserved populations or to public schools" (1993: 13). I have pondered on this issue as my own library debates whether to offer e-mail accounts for a fee to the general public and public employees. Will local e-mail and Internet accounts become a basic necessity for library customer communications with library staff on the status of their records, in getting help for catalog searching, or even for self-placed document delivery transactions, such that it will need to become a basic, perhaps free service? If this were to be the case, limits obviously would have to be set, just as "free accounts" on some free-nets or other civic networks now do not permit such functions as file transfer.

In its frontline role as defender and guarantor of intellectual freedom, the public library may be put in the position of seeming to limit access to information by requiring payment for e-mail accounts. If libraries offer e-mail accounts for a fee, will they be inadvertently reinforcing a two-tiered level of service, based on ability to pay for access to certain information effectively available only through e-mail negotiations? Or is this not a problem as long as library customers are able to walk into a local community library to talk with library staff in person?

The third principle is the "Vital Civic Sector. The information infrastructure must have a vital civic sector at its core." In this statement of principle, the need for creating " 'public arenas' or 'electronic commons' in the media landscape" is equated with the earlier establishment of public libraries and public highways (1994: 3).

Today people long for a sense of community. This is hard to achieve, however, in the face of long work hours and even longer commutes, personal job mobility that cuts one off from friends and family, and a host of other reasons. Just as the public library is the first civic amenity a group of newly built neighborhoods will demand from local government as soon as they reach a critical mass of households and people and begin to see themselves as an aggregate "community," so people who begin to communicate with each other online will want to create a "shared commons in cyberspace" ("Keeping Libraries Alive" 1994: 14).

Dedicated computer users may first experience an online community through a private sector commercial computer network such as Prodigy or America Online. After awhile they begin to realize that something is missing—that is, their friends and neighbors and local business or workplace colleagues who are not yet online. This must be a major reason that civic networks and free-nets are blossoming in communities all over the country. These online pioneers (not necessarily those who blazed the first trails over the passes of the Internet in the early years but the ones who have been driving the wagon trains of local bulletin boards) have seen the possibilities of using the computer as a tool to tie their local communities together and are building the missing link in the information infrastructure at the grassroots level. They see the possibilities for connecting themselves as individuals and as members or leaders of their civic organizations or other voluntary associations. When other community institutions join in, citizens will be able to interact directly with the greater civic community—with their elected and appointed officials, with staff in government agencies and educational institutions, and even with entrepreneurs in the business community. By facilitating community networking through the tools of electronic communication, we are building the communications infrastructure at the local level so it will be in place to enable ordinary people in local communities to participate more fully in the national information system when it becomes ubiquitous.

Libraries can contribute greatly to the development of community networks. In fact, the Center for Civic Networking believes that providing access to civic networks has the potential to "revitalize a key civic institution—the public library" enabling libraries "to blossom into community information centers, serving as gateways of opportunity to the world at large" (1993: 4).

The last principle I will touch on is "Privacy. Privacy should be carefully protected and extended." Preserving privacy and confidentiality of borrower records and other personal information always has been basic to the ethics of librarians. As online library systems allow library users to access their own records, they will be able "to inspect and correct data files about them," as suggested in the text of this statement (Telecommunications Policy Roundtable 1994: 3). The ALA statement on "Principles for the Development of the National Information Infrastructure" strengthens this policy with additional cautions recommending: (1) the development of comprehensive privacy policies, setting limits to personal data collected to provide specific services (dangers in use of data on individual interests compiled for Selective Dissemination of Information profiles come to mind), (2) informed consent to sharing data, and (3) keeping transaction data confidential (ALA 1994). Librarians certainly need to be wary of any proposals to share patron files with other libraries. We need to avoid any movement toward a National Electronic Library with customer databases linked by Social Security or library card barcode number.

THE TASKS WE FACE

The year 2000 is almost upon us. Whatever form a National Electronic Library ultimately may take, the mission of libraries, as Penniman suggests, needs to go "beyond document access . . . to help current and future generations of citizens become independent problem solvers—who have available, and know how to use, information tools to address the challenges that face them" (1993: 19). What can and should library leaders, especially public librarians, do to insure that ordinary people will continue to have free access to the information and knowledge they need in order to learn, grow, thrive, and solve their own problems in the twenty-first century?

Public librarians are uniquely positioned in their communities to shoulder leadership responsibilities for four specific tasks. These are: (1) to educate and convince local government to work with the private and independent sectors to plan and build an electronic community infrastructure that serves *all* of its residents; (2) to develop information policies that serve the public interest at local and state levels as well as at the national level; (3) to organize the community to build a civic computing network as useful to its residents as the commercial telephone, cable, and other emerging multimedia segments of the telecommunications system, and as information-enriched as the local, state, and National Electronic Libraries; and (4) to reinvent the public library as a physical entity, providing virtual access in both community and cyberspace.

Of course public librarians are not solely responsible for these tasks and issues, but if we believe there is a library in the future, if we do give a rat's ass about free access to information, we must see ourselves as major players who are ready and willing to take on the leadership role or, at the minimum we must satisfy ourselves that those who are building the local infrastructure see it as a public enterprise for the public good and in the public interest. To be most effective in accomplishing these tasks, it will be necessary to redefine the roles of each type of library and to develop joint initiatives with colleagues in community college or university libraries, as well as with school library media specialists and corporate librarians in the private sector.

If we are to succeed, we also must enlist key leaders in government and community organizations, to make the cause of public access their own. We must reinforce their awareness of the fact that unless local government institutions and organizations are restructured, retrofitted, or completely redesigned and connected with the emerging telecommunications system, our communities and businesses face the fate of the little towns that were bypassed by the national highway system in the 1950s. None of our communities can afford to let that happen.

Educate and Convince Local Government of the Public Interest in an Electronic Community Infrastructure

Hawkins notes that "Where once our economic strength was determined solely by the depths of our ports or the conditions of our roads, today it is determined as well by our ability to move large quantities of information quickly and accurately and by our ability to use and understand this information" (1994: 24). It is our responsibility to work with citizens to convince local elected officials and other key government decision makers that the infrastructure for the electronic village community must serve both public and private sectors and be equitable and accessible to all residents. As fibernets are put in place and switching centers become operational, public policy must mandate that all public buildings are interconnected and reasonable rates are set at a level that public sector services can absorb. As the Center for Civic Networking urges, we must get the local power structure to "understand and respond to the economic and social costs to our society if ubiquitous access to this national multimedia nervous system is impeded by limited visions of telephone and cable companies motivated to maintain entrenched positions in a rapidly evolving marketplace" (1993: ii). Local, state, and federal telecommunications policy and law must offer both rewards and penalties to reinforce a sense of civic responsibility on the part of the private sector for the broadest access possible.

Fortunately many in the telecommunications industry see a business advantage in universal access—it can only open up new markets. The design and development of the Blacksburg Electronic Village by farsighted leaders at Bell Atlantic in cooperation with the Virginia Polytechnic Institute and State University and the town council offers a hopeful model for civic consensus on the public benefits as well as the business potential of a system that is open to all. Fiber optic cables were laid throughout Blacksburg, high-speed ISDN (Integrated Services Digital Network) lines were installed in all homes, and Ethernet connected all apartment complexes, at no cost to the town. Now everyone who can afford $8.60 a month receives complete electronic services, and those who cannot afford to pay can use public access workstations and get help in the town library. Small businesses are posting their hours, menus, products, and services online, and a florist has already received an order from another country (Bowers 1995: 49–53).

Some public libraries already offer free reference and information services to the small business owner with limited overhead and heavy start-up costs; they need long overdue recognition of their already significant contributions to the economic life of the community. Some libraries have been successful by offering and publicizing small business seminars and other highly visible services designed to introduce entrepreneurs to the online environment. Special fee-based library services that go beyond the basic free level also can provide a highly valued, if partially subsidized, service at reasonable cost for investors or marketers too busy to conduct their own research. Marketed effectively, such services may be the means to convince larger corporations that public investment in the information infrastructure should include the public library as well as other tax-supported public services.

Public librarians need to join forces with local economic development agencies and high-technology councils to earn "a place at the table" by demonstrating the drawing power of an excellent public library system for businesses seeking to relocate, and the direct support libraries can provide new businesses seeking the information they need to survive the competition. Public libraries already connected internationally through systems such as CARL can identify critical intelligence to enrich economic development programs designed to increase local markets' export share or to help the local economic development agency capture local subsidiaries of foreign companies.

In addition to offering business services, public librarians that develop extensive personal networks through active involvement in chambers of commerce and other business and civic organizations can exercise real influence in the power structures of the communities they serve. Broad civic awareness of the public library's basic mission to provide free and equitable access to everyone can lay a foundation for acceptance of the need to preserve this public good in the electronic information environment as well.

Develop Local Public Interest Information Policies

At the national level, librarians have been moderately effective in influencing federal information policy as it relates to maintaining public access to government documents and information in print as well as new formats. Even though in the late 1970s the American Library Association took an early lead in calling for a national information policy, librarians have not been major players in shaping national information policy. We can take heart at the inclusion of at least one library leader in the National Information Infrastructure Advisory Council. Other positive signs include ALA's leadership in the development of the public interest policies discussed earlier, and the broad professional leadership exhibited by the eighteen major library associations that make up the Telecommunications and Information Infrastructure Policy Forum.

ALA's Goal 2000, a five-year plan "to position the Association for the Information Age" recently proposed by Elizabeth Martinez, is probably the most significant sign of hope for librarians (Gaughan 1995: 17). With a new Office of Technology attached to the ALA Washington Office, librarians will have a much stronger base from which to influence information policy development at the national level.

However, at the state level the development of public information policy has been slow; at the local level, it has been practically nonexistent. Only a few states have developed such policies. Maryland's Information Technology Board currently is drafting a policy to guide the management and use of information throughout state and local government.

Since local government is a subdivision of state government and its jurisdictions are chartered and receive their local powers only by state authorization, it follows that local information policy would develop only after the state has initiated the process. Yet, in at least one instance, one local public agency has had reason to develop local information policy, even if it may not have been recognized at the time as such. As early as 1984 in Montgomery County, MD, the Department of Public Libraries developed its "Policy on Basic and Fee-Based Library Services," which has since been revised and updated several times. Its purpose was to define a broad-ranging basic level of library services that would be provided free to all, and to insure that a second level of fee-based services would allow the library to offer enhanced services, defined in this case as limited to highly specialized online database services that would provide nonreusable, private benefits primarily to the individual. The library developed this policy as much to preserve free public library services as to enable it to offer fee-based services and thus remain viable in the electronic environment. The policy satisfied the powerful and vocal advocates of privatization who would have preferred a policy of charging for *all* library services, much as the director of the Baltimore County Public Library now envisions.

The policy also served as a vehicle to communicate with the State Department of Education Division of Library Development and Services on the need for a revision of the state bylaws governing public libraries under which charging fees for any services was illegal. This change eventually was accomplished through an interpretation in state regulations that established almost all public library services as basic and therefore to be provided without direct charge to the user, but allowed all public libraries in the state to offer a second level of fee-based services with limits similar to those established in Montgomery County.

What is instructive about this example is that while the library's fee policy was developed within the framework of local government policy on fees, contracting out, and privatization of government services, no one, including the library director, felt the need at that time to broaden and extend the department level policy as a county government information policy. This reflects the fact that the public library was ten years ahead of other county agencies and was the only agency offering electronic services. Only now are such local government agencies as information systems and telecommunications and environmental protection beginning to explore the issues of whether the public should have free public access or should pay fees for county-developed geographic information system or construction permit information. The need to get the county legal code online mirrors the state-level need to provide online public access to state law through the new Maryland state library network—the rights to which essentially were given away years ago to a private publisher! Librarians may be the only professionals who are even aware of the public policy issues in cases like this, but we often have been late in articulating the public interest and for various reasons still seem hesitant to take up the cloak of leadership through our state professional associations to insure free and equitable access to public information for which the taxpayer has already paid.

The time is now for us to propose and help shape local government information policies that promote citizen access to locally developed information. We must also promote system compatibility and interconnectivity and encourage the design of systems that require little or no learning time. It is to our advantage to offer the public library as free access sites or as sites for consumer testing of new products developed by other government agencies. We also need to link these databases to our public access catalogs for even broader public use.

Organize the Community to Build the Civic Network

Civic computing networks, also called "free-nets," are nonprofit community information services that are volunteer created, governed and managed. They are being organized all across the country, usually under the sponsorship of an academic institution or local government, and often with librarians as instigators or founding members. Librarians are well positioned to accept the challenge of organizing the community to build local and regional networks that can provide new tools for self-governance and give the citizen, as an individual and as a member of voluntary associations or civic organizations, a potentially powerful and effective voice in solving community problems and meeting individual needs.

Public librarians should be involved in building these networks, but their role may vary in different communities. The Cleveland Public Library was an early adopter in making the Cleveland Free-Net available as a menu option on the library's public access catalog, and probably inspired many librarians online across the country to do likewise. In Omaha, Pasadena, and Broward County, the public library founded and hosts the local free-net, providing basic equipment and staff support as an auxiliary library service.

The Illinois Valley Library System received federal funding in 1990 for its P.A.T.H. (Public Access to the Heartland) project, aimed at bringing electronic information to 24 rural and underserved communities in the Peoria area. Bryn Geffert's report in *Public Libraries* (1993: 95) notes that the project was not a complete success, in part because of varying levels of staff commitment to the project in participating libraries. While some actively promoted the P.A.T.H. service and prominently displayed the terminals, others hid the computers or did not even plug them in. While lack of technical know-how may have been the real reason for this, part of the problem may have been that the service was seen either as a threat or as a novelty add-on, rather than as a vital, potentially powerful new tool for libraries.

Geffert reviews the possible uses of the community network in library services, including access to news services and "full text" books and documents.

He sees great value in giving library patrons an introduction to electronic mail which was still new to most people in the early 1990s, and still may be to many (1993: 95). I would speculate that Geffert's failure to see the potential of libraries to free-net discussion groups and bulletin boards may reflect a project goal—bringing "rural and small libraries into the information loop" (1993: 95)—that overlooks a more active role for the library in cultivating individuals and organizations as sources of local and civic information to be shared with the community through the bulletin board and news group format.

Geffert's report on Illinois Valley's pioneering but short-lived "electronic reference desk" best illustrates the need for librarians to see civic networks not "as a replacement for any library service, but as a tool that, with more work and funding, might enable libraries to complement existing services while providing new ones" (1993: 95–96). Staffed only by volunteer librarians on their own time, the reference desk quickly became so popular that it had to be discontinued. At that time, few librarians would have had the computer skills to handle this new task, so the work probably fell on the shoulders of only one or two individuals. For such a service to succeed, the tasks must be "off desk" and on library time, and eventually must be incorporated into the normal work responsibilities of the reference staff.

One must conclude that the Illinois Valley online reference project failed only because it was ahead of its time. A more recent project on CapAccess, the National Capital Area Public Access Network in Washington, D.C., is successful because the work is shared by librarians from ten libraries and is done on paid time. The service was initiated in 1993 by a task force of technical services and reference librarians convened the year before at the request of the directors of the twelve public libraries that provide cooperative services through the Washington Metropolitan Council of Governments. The CapAccess "Reference Q & A" file is listed under the Library Center and is intended to provide answers to factual questions posted by CapAccess members. If research is requested, the member is advised to visit a local library. If the question is unclear, staff communicate with the inquirer via e-mail for clarification. One of the participating librarians from Montgomery County, Brian Auger, reports that each staff member assigned to the service spends only about one hour a month researching the answers and posting them on CapAccess (1994–1995: 6). Libraries contributing staff time to the project include Prince George's and Montgomery county libraries in Maryland, the D.C. Public Library, and the Alexandria Public, Arlington, Fairfax, Falls Church, Loudon, and Prince William county libraries in northern Virginia.

Librarians who have been involved in developeing the CapAccess project agree that among several benefits to libraries, they see this service as "fostering a good relationship between libraries and an emerging patron group." Computer users with modems may not be traditional library customers (1994–1995: 6).

As noted in both the Blacksburg Electronic Village and Illinois Valley Heartland projects, public libraries can make a unique contribution to the civic network by providing basic computer orientation and free access to public workstations in library sites convenient to people who want to become computer literate but who cannot afford a personal computer in their homes or at work. This "safety net" function may be the most important supportive role public libraries can play over the next few years. In partnership with the civic networks, public libraries can help to broaden the network's reach to people who are not computer literate.

Even if the library does not serve as a host or incubator site, is not a founding member of the community network, or cannot yet find the funds to install public access workstations or provide basic training in the library, librarians can still play a leadership role in helping the network to reach out to community organizations and associations, recruiting them as active members, volunteers, and contributors or system managers of online discussion groups or information services.

Finding the staff time to do this may be difficult for librarians already under pressure from cutbacks and other consequences of the recent and ongoing recession. This is one area where volunteers from library boards, friends groups, or recruited at large could be mobilized by the library director and branch managers. Volunteers could be encouraged to use their connections to extend the civic network to their own organizations and neighborhood groups. I believe this is the next best step that public librarians could take to help the cash-strapped, nonprofit civic networks, existing on grants and voluntary donations, to broaden their membership bases, achieve some financial security, and become an even more integral part of the community.

Finally, librarians should be concerned with enriching the content and improving the quality of the information online through the community network. Local government information should be brought online and kept current by the public information office. Through two-way connections between the civic network and local public access catalogs, enhanced by a gateway to the statewide library network, librarians can open additional doors to external information resources and, at the same time, contribute richly diverse and unique local community resources to the national information system that is our shared public enterprise.

Reinvent the Public Library in Community and Cyberspace

The final task public librarians must take on is to reinvent the public library as a virtual enterprise, to provide access for all its constituents both in a physical place in each community and in cyberspace. I believe that as long as books continue to be published and bookstores sign long-term leases, people will want to get their hands on physical collections in a full range of formats. They will continue to demand library buildings conveniently located, open six or seven days a week including evenings and weekends, and fully accessible to everyone.

I do not believe that "cocooning" will become a predominant 24-hour-a-day way of life for most people, or that the individual, no matter how well wired, will somehow get over the need to get out of the house, to physically meet and talk with other human beings. While home schooling is praiseworthy, I do not see the "deschooling of society" any time soon. I cannot believe that most parents, even if they work at home, will want to spend day and night with their kids from infancy until they leave as adults! My hunch is that both home-based entrepreneurs and people who telecommute either full-or part-time will demand community libraries even closer to their homes than we are building now, for the same reasons—conservation of natural resources, air quality, saving time— they employ to justify working at home in the first place!

While a majority still will prefer to borrow books for pleasure reading, I believe that most information that people need to go about their daily lives— making decisions, solving problems, getting directions, learning new tasks, answering questions of fact—will be available (probably by the year 2001) in its most current and accurate form digitally and online. I also believe that much of this "daily bread" information will not be accessible in any other format. Libraries must adapt to this fact of life, as many already have begun to do by reallocating a portion of library materials budgets from print purchases to digital access license fees for journal indexes, full-text periodicals, and reference tools.

There is no question that libraries must "learn as rapidly as possible how to use new information technology to provide ever-increasing value" to our customers. As futurist David Snyder recently advised the Montgomery County library:

Eventually, electronic tele-computing technology will perform most public contact functions of libraries. For the near-term future, however—the next ten years at least—our electronic info-structure will still be maturing, and the general public's computer competency will still be limited, even as the public's need for new knowledge and skills required by general participation in the informated marketplace and the workplace will be rapidly expanding. Thus, the public's utility for traditional library functions in traditional library settings can be expected to grow even as we invent the new 'cybrary' of the 21st Century. (Snyder 1994: 3)

What does all this imply for the library as a physical entity, and for the library as an organization? What needs to change? What needs to remain the same? While I do not presume to have the answers, I do have a few intuitive guesses and some ideas picked up from reading or borrowed from colleagues.

The Library Building

Libraries will continue to bring resources to people through a decentralized network of library buildings, each conveniently located at the hub of a community. Even as remote electronic access to library information resources becomes more readily available, libraries will need to be open longer hours so that customers can actually use or borrow media and print materials, and also gain access to public workstations. Whether library buildings will need to be larger or smaller, space allocation will be quite different.

Print reference collections definitely will be smaller as more tools are published only in digital format. Circulating collections may be smaller too, as local and statewide library networks provide information about additional library resources elsewhere that can be easily borrowed (provided that we are able to improve turnaround time for physical delivery and that "net lending libraries" do not become more reluctant to share their materials through interlibrary loan). Best sellers and other current books in both hardcover and paper still will need prominent display space. However, the format of some popular, current books may move more to audiotape, probably in digital compressed form, and will be in much demand by those who are still commuting. Library customers are already demanding books in CD-ROM format for use on home computers. Libraries will need to accommodate other new formats that even now are being invented in the basements and garages of the world. At some point in the future, libraries may serve as sites for databanks from which borrowers can download the full text of books onto smart cards.

As formats multiply and rapid changes continue, buildings will need to be designed for more flexible use. Single, large, barrier-free open areas will allow for adaptations for future technology and maximum self-service. Shelving systems will accommodate a shifting mix of formats and security systems will protect all kinds of materials. Any space that may be saved by smaller book and media collections will be reallocated for public access workstations. In fact, computers and printers will fill any available space not otherwise occupied. Some terminals will be dedicated to specific uses such as self-charge and maybe self-check-in, or for searching the local public access catalog. Others will be multipurpose for those who require access to a full range of library resources and optional functions. Software adaptations and furniture accommodations for people with disabilities will be installed on some if not all workstations. Accommodations will be made to charge for paper printouts, though a certain number of pages may be provided free to library card holders.

Small conference rooms will be needed for hands-on training and personal tutoring by volunteers or library staff in computer literacy or computer-assisted reading programs. Special spaces for use of portable personal computers, with noise baffles from larger public areas, will allow individuals to manipulate information from databases downloaded at the library.

Large meeting rooms, fully wired with satellite access, will meet the community's need for "face time" and offer places for libraries to host teleconferences for staff continuing education and for use by local community groups, including activists organizing the civic network.

While new information technology applications may call for larger buildings, fiscal constraints probably will keep the size of new libraries constant. This would force more frequent discarding of books and transfer to optical storage of standard and older holdings such as periodical back runs, including digital versions no longer stored in computer memory on the public access catalog.

A basic requirement is that all public libraries be connected through fibernet to the community information infrastructure, to all school media centers and libraries in colleges and universities, and to other corporate entities in the jurisdiction or beyond.

The Cybrary

As we design and build the local components of the National Electronic Library, we need to consider how to translate the local library as a physical entity into its digital incarnation online. I envision a "sim library" mirroring each community library's physical structure that would serve as a three-dimensional map of the building. By using the "point and click" method, the simulation could provide entry points into various aspects of the collection, staff resources, and the surrounding neighborhoods.

For new buildings, it should be possible to obtain the architect's computer-assisted design program on which to paint the full picture of the completed library and all its resources. The library simulation could become a basic building block in an overall "sim community," akin to M. Strata Rose's science fiction-sounding image of the "Virtual City" she is designing. "The network of crystal walkways that thread the city go both above and below. Graceful arches span the great towers, thread the atrium, meander along the chasms of the Farside Trench." It may be a stretch to imagine the library in this way, but I would like this virtual public library to be as inviting as Rose's "new, cool, undiscovered coffee shop on the net to hang out in" (Fjermedal 1995: 61).

The CARL Corporation's Kid's Catalog, that includes a map of the library shelves with a device that blinks to identify shelf location, provides a preview of the simulated multimedia environment. As in Rose's vision, the sim library could be populated. For example, you would enter the program and find yourself walking up to the library and pushing the front door open, where you would be greeted by the community librarian who would thank you for coming and then announce the actual library hours. Moving inside and up to the circulation desk, a person could see and hear a recording by the circulation supervisor on how to use the selfo-charge machine or how to access one's borrowing record. A user would scan the bookshelves to see where the mysteries or travel books were located, and might then point to the "Librarian's Choice" shelf, where staff traditionally display lesser known but highly recommended authors. With a click, a librarian would come up with a brief booktalk on one or two titles or a series by a specific writer, followed by directions to the catalog and how to place a hold. Kids in neighborhood schools could be invited to participate with their own recommendations for "good reads," and invite others to attend a junior great books discussion group meeting at the library every Wednesday evening (or an online conference on the community network, for that matter!). Some libraries might offer home delivery for a requested item, and build into this simulation the capability of charging the service fee to a personal credit card.

This simulation could include the capability of moving to the library system level, with the library board president or the library director recording a brief message about the current state of the budget or a new strategic plan. This could be followed by a request for feedback using another button that would get the customer into the budget or planning document itself, with directions on how to comment on proposed priorities. The possibilities are endless!

I can even see the branch manager working with a local chamber of commerce to build a simulation of the neighborhood adjacent to the library, visualizing nearby bookstores, restaurants, and other businesses. To promote the library's summer reading program, the local McDonald's in the simulation could offer coupons for ambitious readers (printed out then and there in the library), or the computer store could sponsor one of the workstations in the library. In exchange, the simulation would display a notice about the store's latest software packages along with a public service message in support of the library's business services. This may be much too commercial for traditionalist librarians, but public/private partnerships are probably the only way a library can afford to build such a guide. The library would also need to work closely with its parent jurisdiction; it would be worth exploring to see if the community segment of the simulation could be based on the geographic information system that many cities and counties now are designing.

Since all this is only a fantasy at this point, the obvious questions are how will libraries get the upfront money to invest in the equipment and software to create the sim library, and how will the necessary staff expertise be found to keep it up-to-date so that the illusion of reality can be maintained. Partnerships have been suggested; grants might be a possibility for pilot projects. As to expertise, we all know that somewhere there is a twelve-year-old who could do all this right now! I am counting on that person to grow up, join the library staff, and take us to the next level. In the meantime, we will have to do the best we can, with the staff and the leadership we now have, to reinvent the library organization as well.

The Library Organization

Given all the changes implied in the images above, it becomes clear that the library organization will have to be structured as a learning society. Constant change and reorganization will be a way of life. Librarians finally will develop management information systems to help them constantly evaluate the quality and impact of customer services. Staff participation will be encouraged in decisions that affect their work, and they will be involved in the redesign of service delivery as needs change and financial challenges continue.

Reference functions will be "informated" to a great extent, with selected librarians servicing two-way voice, video, and text workstations located in community agencies and businesses. A centralized telephone reference service could handle this, but it might be useful to consider branch staff interacting with selected locations in their library service areas. They would need the capability of switching to staff in other libraries or information resources for special subject expertise or calling up online resources from the civic network, local library catalog, and state library network as needed. As suggested in the scenario above, they would need to negotiate the reference interview either online or in an interactive video format, with online users who have pushed the help button.

More functions will be contracted out, especially one-time tasks such as new system installations, database development, and maintenance. Much of what has been traditional collection development functions may be handled by vendors or shared interactively between central and branch staff in an online mode. "High end" fee-based services may be contracted to the private sector in a virtual library partnership and profit-sharing enterprise.

Productivity improvements through information technology and "working smarter" will allow the library to keep up with increases in use with few or no additional staff. Library support staff will carve out new roles and niches in service delivery, probably acquiring the "tech expert" role in troubleshooting systems that a few librarians now fill mostly by default because no one else knows how. Many technical support staff will telecommute at least part-time. Libraries will need to expand and nurture their volunteer cadres and bring in people with computer skills and fund-raising capabilities.

Job responsibilities will be flexible and evolve continually, but in some cases will change in very short time periods. Library staff constantly will have to learn new skills, such as communicating through recorded messages and keeping a local simulation up-to-date, as described above. Managers will be expected to develop good community relations skills with all kinds of groups and their leaders. Staff at all levels probably will need more off-desk time for continual upgrading of skills and continuing education in new subject areas as well as emerging technologies.

Staff will become accustomed to direct online e-mail communications with each other and with line managers up to and including the director. Facilitating group processes and interpersonal communications skills will be tops on the training agenda for work groups, task forces, leadership teams, and labor-management councils. Working in the library that functions as a learning society will not be easy. Participation in management does not bring utopia—in fact, it can be very disturbing for some people. But unless the library is able to bring all of its staff along, and make full use of everyone's ideas, including those of the library's constituents, the library and its services will not remain relevant and useful.

At the local level just as much as at the national level, librarians must reinvent themselves and the library services they provide, keeping the traditional approaches and materials when they still meet people's needs. But above all, in whatever we do, we must make sure that citizens continue to have free and equitable access to the information they need, that they are able to communicate freely and without violation of privacy, and that the new communications infrastructure serves the whole community.

CONCLUSION

Our responsibility as librarians is to work with our citizens and with each other as colleagues to build the National Electronic Library, not as some kind of superorganized hierarchical structure but more like the Internet that has come into existence as much by happenstance as by design. We are not really building a national library but weaving a loosely knit learning web. This "integrated fabric of knowledge services" (Young 1994: 112) grows out of its separate elements: national consortia and associations of libraries, national and regional bibliographic utilities, state library networks, city and county library systems, and local components including the civic networks, community libraries, school and college media centers, the branches of research and university libraries, and corporate libraries.

It is all part of a national enterprise that is creating the public and private communications infrastructure to support the emerging knowledge society. Libraries are not the biggest players, but they provide a major component of the information base of the system. Librarians are entrusted with the mission of insuring that public interest principles and the public good are served through this public enterprise.

I have focused on the tasks of public librarians at the local level: to work with local government to build the community infrastructure, to develop local information policies based on public interest principles, to organize the community to build the civic networks, and to reinvent the library in community and in cyberspace.

If we can accomplish all this, or at least be sure we are well on our way, then we will be able to focus on the really critical issues for society as a whole. We need to think about the future of literacy and reading, not about books; the future of free access, not about libraries; the future of thinking and civil discourse, not about government. We need to keep these concerns in mind as we create the National Electronic Library as our contribution to the public enterprise.

REFERENCES

American Library Association. 1994. Telecommunications and Information Infrastructure Policy Forum. "Principles for the Development of the National Information Infrastructure." (brochure)

Auger, Brian. 1994–1995. "Virtual Reference Service in the D.C. Area." *The Crab: The Maryland Library Association Newsletter* 25 (Winter): 6.

Bowers, John. 1995. "Wiring Dixie." *NetGuide* 2 (January): 48–53.

Campbell, Jerry D. 1993. "Choosing to Have a Future." *American Libraries* 24 (June): 560–566.

Center for Civic Networking. 1993. *A National Strategy for Civic Networking: A Vision of Change.* Washington, DC: Center for Civic Networking.

Dowlin, Kenneth E. 1993. "The Neographic Library: A 30 Year Perspective on Public Libraries." In *Libraries and the Future: Essays on the Library in the Twenty-First Century*, ed. F. W. Lancaster. New York: Haworth Press, 29–43.

Fjermedal, Grant. 1995. "The Tomorrow Makers." *NetGuide* 2 (January): 55–67.

Gaughan, Tom. 1995. "ALA Goal 2000: Planning for the Millenium." *American Libraries* 26 (January): 17–21.

Geffert, Bryn. 1993. "Community Networks in Libraries: A Case Study of the Freenet P.A.T.H." *Public Libraries* 32 (March/April): 91–99.

Hawkins, Brian L. 1994. "Planning for the National Electronic Library." *Educom Review* 29: 19–29.

Jackson, Joab. 1995. "The Mad Librarian." *Baltimore* 88 (January): 49–50.

"Keeping Libraries Alive." 1994. *The Economist* 332 (August 27): 14.

Montgomery County (Maryland) Department of Public Libraries. 1984. "Policy on Basic and Fee-Based Services." Rockville, MD: Montgomery County Government.

Montgomery County (Maryland) Department of Public Libraries. 1995. *Creating a Vision for the Future: Strategic Plan for Public Libraries in Montgomery County, Maryland, FY 1996–2001.* Rockville, MD: Montgomery County Government.

Penniman, W. David. 1993. "Visions of the Future: Libraries and Librarianship for the Next Century." The Fifth Nasser Sharify Lecture, Sunday, April 18. New York: Pratt Graduate School of Information and Library Science. (booklet)

Snyder, David Pearce. 1994. "Comments on the Draft Strategic Plan for Public Libraries." Paper submitted to the director of the Montgomery County Department of Public Libraries, November 30.

Telecommunications Policy Roundtable. 1994. *Renewing the Commitment to a Public Interest Telecommunications Policy: Public Interest Principles.* Washington, DC: Telecommunications Policy Roundtable. (leaflet)

Young, Peter R. 1994. "Changing Information Access Economics: New Role for Libraries and Librarians." *Information Technologies and Libraries* 13 (June): 103–114.

5

Library Education and the National Electronic Library

Faye N. Vowell

In a recent article in *The Atlantic Monthly* entitled "The Age of Social Transformation," Peter Drucker offers an interpretation of our present and future in which knowledge is a key resource and inequity in the social order is caused by lack of knowledge.

He describes knowledge workers as people who "require a great deal of formal education and [possess] the ability to acquire and to apply theoretical and analytical knowledge. They require a different approach to work and a different mind-set. Above all, they require a habit of continuous learning" (Drucker 1994: 62).

As Drucker describes the role education will play in training future knowledge workers, he posits that the central concerns of this knowledge society will be twofold: (1) the basic knowledge one must possess and (2) defining quality in teaching and learning. The description of an educated person will no longer be someone who possesses a certain body of knowledge. Instead it will be someone who "has learned how to learn, and who continues learning, especially by formal education, throughout his or her lifetime" (Drucker 1994: 66–67). This concentration on learning could lead to a real democratization of power, making the possibility of leadership open to all; this learning will be enhanced by technology. "Learning will become the tool of the individual—available to him or her at any age—if only because so much skill and knowledge can be acquired by means of the new learning technologies" (Drucker 1994: 67).

The work unit of the future according to Drucker will be the team rather than the individual—with different kinds of teams constituted for different purposes. The information explosion will cause people to become more specialized in their knowledge and instead of one knowledge there will be many knowledges. "The understanding of teams, the performance capacities of different kinds of teams, their strengths and limitations, and the tradeoffs between various kinds of teams will thus become central concerns in the management of people" (Drucker 1994: 68). These work teams must be associated with an organization to be effective because the organization converts the specialized knowledge of the different teams into a product. Management then becomes a crucial function of the organization.

In *The Age of the Network: Organizing Principles for the 21st Century* (1994: xvii), Jessica Lipnack and Jeffrey Stamps extend this thinking about the importance of teams:

With change as the underlying driver, organizations need more speed and flexibility, greater scope and sharper intelligence, more creativity and shared responsibility. Teams offer part of the answer. . . . Networks—of teams and other groups joined together which we call "teamnets"—offer another, newer part of the answer.

Drawing on Alvin Toffler's 1980 book, *The Third Wave*, they hypothesize that in the First Age, the Nomadic, the basic organizational unit was the small group. The second age, the Agricultural, is characterized by hierarchy as its basic organization. In the third age, the Industrial, bureaucracy was the organizational principle. In the current age, the Information Age, the predominant organization is the network. Interestingly this "electronic network" metaphor for the information age is being applied in a number of contexts: as a form of both social and business organization and to describe the physical infrastructure of the Internet. The image of a network is permeating all levels and aspects of society. Networking is also emphasized in John Naisbitt's *Megatrends* and *Megatrends 2000*.

Librarians are knowledge workers in this Age of Information; they can and should play a key role in helping their publics meet the challenges inherent in the utilization of information which forms the basis of their knowledge. As educators who prepare these librarians, administrators and faculty members in schools of library and information studies (LIS) must be aware of the latest technological developments that shape access to and dissemination of information, in addition to keeping abreast of the new pedagogies for delivering this knowledge. We must update our curricula and conceptions of the skills and knowledge our graduates need to be successful. As Richard B. Heydinger expressed in the draft of his lead article for the October/November 1994 issue of *On the Horizon*, "Twenty first century higher education must become mission-driven, customer sensitive, enterprise-organized, and results oriented" (1994:1).

NATIONAL ELECTRONIC LIBRARY

A new era in access to and dissemination of information was signaled by James H. Billington, the Librarian of Congress, in his remarks at the National Digital Library news conference when he unveiled a partnership between the Packard Foundation, the Kellogg Foundation, Metromedia, and the Library of Congress. This partnership will make available in a digitized format 5 million unique items in American history by the turn of the century (Billington 1995: 89). In Billington's own words,

We believe that the National Digital Library, properly organized and supported, with its capacity for sharing knowledge and information now confined to the great research depositories like the Library, can directly enrich the possibilities of our schools, libraries, universities and research institutes and the millions of Americans who use them. (Billington 1994: 413)

The Library already makes available 26 million bibliographic records, as well as materials from major exhibits and six collections of American history holdings; these can be accessed free of charge using the Internet (Billington 1995: 89).

These efforts by the Library to make resources available electronically are echoed by numerous other consortia and private organizations and individuals. New electronic journals come into being daily; "listservs" and bulletin boards increase our access to new information exponentially. On local and regional levels, librarians in research, public, and special libraries and information centers are working to create virtual libraries or electronic libraries which emulate the national effort. Pamela Jajko describes such a virtual library as follows:

An entity for knowledge management that effectively incorporates both the traditional library domain and the use of both telecommunication and computer technology to facilitate the rapid access and use of information by individual users through the apparently seamless integration of knowledge from that library's own resources, from internal, proprietary information of that library's organization and from external, worldwide information sources. (1993: 52)

She offers the following twelve premises underlying any effort to create a virtual library on the local level.

1. Information is a critical resource.
2. Information differs.
3. Information will coexist in print and electronic format.
4. Information must be organized.
5. Information must be planned and managed globally.

6. The end user will be the focus.

7. Technology will advance.

8. Customization will create the customer base.

9. Standards such as the Z39.50 protocol will enable information exchange.

10. Quality is integral to all operations.

11. Ethical guidelines are essential.

12. Laws such as intellectual property rights and copyright law must be understood and followed.

LIS educators must know how to use the tools of the virtual or electronic library and train their students to become proficient in using them and the information they contain to serve their future clients. Our graduates must also understand the underlying premises that Jajko articulates and the problem-solving strategies that are implicit in their statement as they attempt to bring their own libraries into the 21st century.

NEW TEACHING AND LEARNING ENVIRONMENT

The same technology that makes the National Electronic Library possible has also given birth to a new teaching and learning environment. In a recent *Educom Review* article, Carol Twigg calls for the creation of a national learning infrastructure (NLI), a new paradigm in teaching and learning. This NLI is made possible by a variety of technology-mediated learning environments "including stand-alone, computer assisted instruction (CAI) applications; networked information resources; experimentation via new modes of communication (e.g., computer conferencing); and distance learning developed by both individual institutions and consortial or statewide efforts and offered primarily, though not exclusively, via television." Twigg's proposed national learning infrastructure would "simultaneously increase access (via the network), improve quality (through the availability of individualized, interactive learning materials), and contain costs (by reducing labor intensity in instruction)" (Twigg 1994: 23).

To meet the challenge of this kind of learning environment, libraries and library schools must become learning organizations like those Peter Senge describes in *The Fifth Discipline* (1990). Michael E. McGill and John W. Slocum, Jr., expand Senge's definition to a discussion of a smarter organization which

facilitates the learning of all of its members and continuously transforms itself. Learning is not training. Training involves putting information in front of people and encouraging them to use it. Learning encourages people to wonder and figure out things on their own in order to improve their organization's effectiveness. It includes letting people try out these new behaviors and occasionally make a mistake. Often these mistakes create opportunities for real learning to happen. (1994: 10)

To remain viable in a changing economic and social climate, libraries and library schools have to have the flexibility and creativity that will come from becoming such smarter learning organizations. The benefits of doing so will be apparent in the policies and procedures of both organizations and in the skills and abilities of the librarians they produce. A culture will be created that is open to experience and encourages responsible risk-taking. The rites, rituals, heroes, and legends of the organization will give testimony to these values; all the stakeholders will feel they have opportunities to learn and grow (McGill and Slocum 1994: 13).

As the library of the future will not be defined by bricks and mortar, neither will LIS education. Distance delivery through interactive television, using the Internet, and by faculty traveling to teach at off-campus, even out-of-state and out-of-country, sites will be increasingly common as we employ in our teaching the technology our students will use in meeting the information needs of their clients.

Ernest A. DiMattia, Jr., has addressed one aspect of this distance delivery in ''Total Quality Management and Servicing Users through Remote Access Technology.'' In looking toward the future, DiMattia sees that:

The concept of off-hours, off-site availability of information will become the norm and more providers of information will seek methods of offering their indexes, abstracts and texts whenever, wherever and however users will require. The successful providers will be those who heed the need of the customer by offering the best service at the best cost the best way. The merging of remote technological access, needed information sources, and total quality management will achieve the kind of results which will ensure a more positive . . . relationship. (1993: 191)

This quote is instructive in a number of ways. First, in our distance delivery of education we need to provide the same kind of off-hours, off-site access to information to support our students' learning that we will expect them to provide their own clients in a library setting. We have an opportunity to model a high standard of service and an understanding of individual learning styles and information needs. The truism that faculty teach the way they were taught probably holds true with librarians, who have as their standard of service the service they themselves received.

Another interesting distance learning strategy is the creation of virtual communities of learners using electronic networks. By doing so, we can offer avenues of learning that are enhanced by using technology. Activities such as cooperative and collaborative learning benefit from the flexibility of using networked technology. Students can interact through direct instruction, real-time conversation, time-delayed conversation, and learning by doing (Ehrmann 1990 cited in Kurshan, Harrington, and Milbury 1994). As our students learn in such virtual communities, they will absorb the ancillary benefit of experiencing how such communities are created and function. In the course of their careers as information professionals, they will have opportunities to create virtual communities themselves—either in the workplace or in support of clients. Kurshan, Harrington, and Milbury's *An Educator's Guide to Electronic Networking: Creating Virtual Communities* (1994) is a good place to begin exploration of this topic.

An even more visionary use of technology to enhance LIS education is that offered through the use of multimedia to create virtual reality. Christopher Dede predicts that in the next ten years:

the fusion of computers and telecommunications will lead to the development of highly realistic virtual environments that are collaborative and interactive. [Multimedia can foster] a new model of teaching/learning based on learners' navigation and creation of knowledge webs [evolving] structured inquiry approaches that build on web-like architectures from hypermedia. . . . Such an evolution would make multimedia the core of an information infrastructure that could be a driveshaft for educational reform. (1992: 54)

Virtual reality could have a dynamic and exciting impact on education. As Sandra Helsel predicts:

Learning via printed symbols in textbooks will shift to learning via simulations. . . . Curriculum materials will no longer be predominantly text-based, but will be imagery and symbol-based. Virtual reality has the potential to move education from its reliance on textbook abstractions to experiential learning in naturalistic settings. (1992: 41)

The possibility of participating in a simulated event could have a tremendous impact on student learning.

Widespread use of such a teaching technology would also greatly influence the ways as well as the kind of information that is stored and retrieved. In the future, information seekers will need to access databases, moving images and pictures as frequently as they do text. The web-like architecture that Dede calls for is a more flexible way of storing and retrieving data that can be individualized to a user's specific learning style and needs. Our graduates may find themselves supporting a teacher in designing such a virtual reality classroom for a younger student or adult learner taking such a class.

In this same vein, Lauren H. Seiler, a sociology professor at Queens College in the City University of New York (CUNY) system, describes a second wave of change whereby electronic books and libraries will be augmented by other methods of information storage:

Databases, to a greater extent, will complement the functions of electronic libraries and the notions of database and library will merge. Electronic books will replace their print counterparts but even electronic books will be largely superseded by databases, the reactive media [television, records, video], the interactive multimedium [computer games], and virtual reality. Finally the [digital electronic medium] will give way to a medium based on light (photons)—the digital photonic medium. (1992: 19).

LIS professionals will need to create easy user interfaces to collections of such information. What better way to gain familiarity with this application than to experience it in the library science classroom?

Yet, our MLS graduates will need to possess the skills to use technology as a tool to achieve their ends, not as an end in itself. Even now, Robert C. Heterick and John Gehl (1995: 25) predict a time when computer and communications technologies won't be tools anymore because they will be the environment.

CURRICULA

As we look to this future, LIS curricula will need to be flexible and responsive to changing information needs. We will have to better coordinate degree-related and continuing education offerings while equipping individuals to be change agents within their organizations. This change is particularly frightening and frustrating, for instance, as new technology appears on the scene before we have become totally familiar with the current technology. See Jane E. Klobas (1990) for a discussion of "Managing Technological Change in Libraries and Information Services." Ross Atkinson (1992) in "The Acquisitions Librarian as Change Agent in the Transition to the Electronic Library" discusses a productive response to the change which will accompany the advent of the digital library. He suggests that libraries begin to act as publishers themselves taking advantage of the electronic medium. In addition, librarians can forge a link between the library and information engineering:

this is necessary not only to gather the information needed to advise the information engineer on future technical development requirements, but also more fundamentally to ensure that all delivery operations are meeting the needs of scholarly information exchange. (1992: 17)

Our graduates need to be offered opportunities to develop the skills necessary to meet such changes.

Our doctoral graduates will need to possess the skills to create new knowledge for the field by practicing strategic, holistic, interdisciplinary thinking from global, international, and multicultural perspectives. They will need to conduct the research and build the theories and models that practicing librarians can use in their daily professional lives.

As Grover and Greer state, the library of the future will move from its role as a warehouse to that of an information utility with an accompanying shift in focus and values:

While the library as a warehouse values books and the items warehoused, the alternative information utility places value on serving its customers. Since service is the valued commodity, the staff providing service are more important resources than information packages which make up the library collection. (1995: 4)

They continue with the observation that

technology has engendered a global society which transcends traditional barriers of time and space. Most of the information needed by an individual or an enterprise to succeed is accessible through the existing and developing capacities of local, regional, national, and global components of modern information networks. The role of the information utility is to marshall this information and to package it for use locally. (1995: 4)

The concept of the library as an information utility in a larger organization can be applied to the K-12 school library situation as well as the public library. James E. Herring envisions future school libraries as

an important part of the school information system which meets the needs of administrators, teachers, librarians, and pupils for information. The system will provide electronic mail, electronic noticeboards, databases—administrative, library/resources, careers, view databases and links to external databases. The emphasis in schools will be to encourage pupils and staff to *think* about how information is created, searched for, manipulated and used. In short, to create an information environment in the school. (1987: 235–236)

The school librarian in such an organization is an important partner in providing access to information repackaged to serve the needs of a diverse clientele.

With this vision of the library as an information utility and the librarian as a knowledge worker, certain assumptions about the curriculum in library and information management follow logically. Graduates need to have a strong grounding in the philosophical foundations of information transfer and the role of the information professional in society. They need to understand the psychology of information use, the behavioral theories applied to patterns of seeking, processing, and using information in order to design, implement, and evaluate an information system or process sensitive to the behavioral patterns of individuals. Graduates need to be aware of the roles, strategies, and significance of the information transfer process in the diffusion of knowledge. A grasp of the theory of the organization of information is needed as they strive to understand the development and evaluation of theory and practice in the organization and retrieval of information in various formats. Graduates also need an understanding of how to apply managerial theory in the operation of information organizations.

This strong theory base is a necessary prerequisite to more practical or applied learning since it provides the foundation on which to build the habit of continuous learning that Drucker calls for. The combination of theory with tools courses such as information needs analysis, basic information sources, repackaging information, and online searching allows students to acquire and apply the theoretical and analytical knowledge which Drucker also sees as necessary.

In addition to a strong theory base allied with practical or applied learning, our graduates need to possess the necessary people skills to make them capable managers and equally capable team players or participants in teamnets. As S. Michael Malinconico observes in "What Librarians Need to Know to Survive in an Age of Technology," "The rising importance of information and information handling technologies is drawing librarians ever more conspicuously into the mainstream of the activities of the organizations they serve" (1992: 234). To accommodate this new role, our graduates need to understand the dynamics of group processes, need to know how to function in bureaucracies, and need to possess superior oral and written communication skills—especially as they explain library goals, objectives, and requirements to nonlibrarians. Our curricula should also enhance students' problem-solving skills and ability to ask the right question, rather than find the right answer.

Raymond F. Vondran concurs in citing a set of basic competencies for the information age drawn from the work of John Naisbitt and Patricia Aburdene: "thinking skills which should be fluid and oriented toward problem solving; communication skills, which are both precise and expressive; and learning skills which will provide the basic adaptive abilities necessary in a changing environment" (1990: 28). Vondran continues to underline the need for "adaptable creative problem-solvers, who will soon develop into effective managers" (1990: 30).

Malinconico echoes Drucker when he emphasizes the importance of teaching our students management skills, especially the distinction between line management and project management. "The acquisition, implementation and operation of the products of modern technology will present librarians with many of their greatest and most intriguing management challenges" (1992: 238). Management of teams of people as well as management of finances and technology are crucial for success in the library of the future.

OUTCOMES ASSESSMENT

The skills and areas of knowledge expected of graduates of a master's program should be articulated in concrete goals statements. For example, graduates could be expected to be able to accomplish the following:

1. to articulate a philosophy of the library and information professions;
2. to recognize basic human behavior patterns applied to the information transfer process;
3. to comprehend the theory of information transfer and general patterns of information transfer in society;
4. to articulate the major methods of organizing information for use in the design and implementation of information systems;
5. to analyze the information needs of a client group;
6. to evaluate and design information systems, employing appropriate methods and technologies;

7. to apply appropriate research methodology and interpret research results in the management of an information system;

8. to manage an information system, employing appropriate management theory; and

9. to design appropriate services for a particular environment based on the comprehension of the societal functions of libraries and information centers (educational, cultural, informational, recreational, and bibliographic). (ESU SLIM Assessment Plan: 1995)

LIS education is subject to the same requirements for accountability that face the rest of education. Accrediting agencies as well as governing boards and legislatures are calling for measures that document that we are providing the education that we say we are. A variety of assessment measures can be used to evaluate the extent to which our graduates achieve such goals as those stated above. Payne, Vowell, and Black (1991) describe the following kinds of assessment:

1. locally developed achievement measures;

2. external expert evaluation;

3. self-reported data collection (surveys, inventories, interviews, panels, student journals, self-assessment classes);

4. nationally standardized achievement tests;

5. persistence studies; and

6. portfolio analysis.

To be successful, assessment programs should be coherent, unified, proactive, and indigenous, and grow out of an institution's culture. Plans should also be low-cost, use what information is currently available whenever possible, provide minimal disruption of faculty patterns, and be integrated with already existing assessment (Payne, Vowell, and Black 1992: 75).

CONTINUING EDUCATION

Although he does not think that the information age will cause the education of librarians to be vastly different from that which "should be properly provided in any other era," John Corbin in "The Education of Librarians in an Age of Information Technology" proposes a partnership between LIS schools and the libraries which hire our graduates:

The professional schools first must provide librarians with a sound foundation of the principles and concepts of library and information science with as many experiences with information processing systems and related technology as possible, taught by knowledgeable faculty. The libraries employing librarians then must contribute to the continuation of their education through a number of well planned and organized programs and techniques such as improved on-the-job training, educational guidance, mentor programs, access to continuing education opportunities, and research and publication programs. (1988: 86)

LIS schools also have a responsibility for continuing education. The technology and distance delivery described above will enable us to offer more of the latest concepts and strategies to more geographically remote areas to keep our graduates up to date. As James E. Rush observes, "since availability of and access to information resources will be common to all libraries and information centers, it will be possible to improve and strengthen the training and continuing education programs of libraries and information centers correspondingly" (1993: 22). He further proposes that we share effort and expertise by not hiring staff at every site to conduct this continuing education; the implication is that such training could be delivered using technology. Finally, continuing education for mid-career librarians is a necessity and responsibility of LIS educators. As knowledge workers, they will need lifelong, formal education on a regular basis.

CONCLUSION

The changes that the National Electronic Library or the national digital library calls for in the way we access, utilize, store, and retrieve information mirror the changes necessary in LIS education as we teach our graduates to be comfortable in this new electronic milieu. But we also need to be responsive to accompanying societal and pedagogical changes and developments. As Don Tapscott and Art Caston observe in *Paradigm Shift: The New Promise of Information Technology*:

There is a new openness and volatility that seem rich with opportunity and fraught with danger for humanity, your country, your organization and you. . . . Information and information technology are at the center of the opening. . . . Global telecommunications networks energize the metabolism of world commerce and move us inexorably toward Marshall McLuhan's global village. (1993: 1–2)

Librarians are key participants in that global village.

REFERENCES

Atkinson, Ross. 1992. "The Acquisitions Librarian as Change Agent in the Transition to the Electronic Library." *Library Resources and Technical Services* 36, no. 1 (January): 7–20.

Billington, James H. 1994. "The Librarian's Remarks at the National Digital Library News Conference." *Library of Congress Information Bulletin* 53, no. 20: 412–413, 416.

Billington, James H. 1995. "The Library and the Information Superhighway." *Civilization* (January/February): 89.

Campbell, J. D. 1993. "Choosing to Have a Future." *American Libraries* 24, no. 6: 560–563.

Corbin, John. 1988. "The Education of Librarians in an Age of Information Technology." *Computing, Electronic Publishing and Information Technology*. New York: Haworth Press.

Dede, Christopher J. 1992. "The Future of Multimedia: Bridging to Virtual Worlds." *Educational Technology* (May): 54–60.

DiMattia, Ernest A., Jr. 1993. "Total Quality Management and Servicing Users through Remote Access Technology." *The Electronic Library* 11, no. 3: 187–191.

Drucker, Peter F. 1994. "The Age of Social Transformation." *The Atlantic Monthly* (November): 53–80.

Ehrmann, S. C. 1992. "Challenging the Ideal of Campus-Bound Education." *Educom Review* 27, no. 2: 22–26.

Emporia State University, School of Library and Information Management. 1995. *Assessment Plan*. Emporia, KS: Emporia State University

Greer, Roger C. 1982. "Information Transfer: A Conceptual Model for Librarianship, Information Science and Information Management." *IATUL Proceedings* 20: 3–10.

Greer, Roger, and Robert Grover. 1995. "Libraries as Public Information Utilities: An Imperative for Survival." Unpublished document.

Helsel, Sandra. 1992. "Virtual Reality and Education." *Educational Technology* (May): 38–42.

Herring, James E. 1987. "The Electronic School Library." *The Electronic Library* 5, no. 4 (August): 230–236.

Heterick, Robert C., Jr., and John Gehl. 1995. "Information Technology and the Year 2020." *Educom Review* (January/February): 23–25.

Heydinger, Richard B. 1994. "A Reinvented Model for Higher Education." Horizons listserv, Wednesday, September 21, 10:23 CST. Morrison@gibbs.oit.unc.edu.

Jajko, Pamela. 1993. "Planning the Virtual Library." *Medical Reference Services Quarterly* 12, no. 3: 51–67.

Klobas, Jane E. 1990. "Managing Technological Change in Libraries and Information Services." *The Electronic Library* 8, no. 5 (October): 344–349.

Kurshan, Barbara L., Marcia A. Harrington, and Peter G. Milbury. 1994. *An Educator's Guide to Electronic Networking: Creating Virtual Communities*. Syracuse, NY: ERIC Clearinghouse on Information & Technology, Syracuse University, IR–96.

Lipnack, Jessica, and Jeffrey Stamps. 1994. *The Age of the Network: Organizing Principles for the 21st Century*. Essex Junction, VT: Oliver Wight Publications.

Malinconico, S. Michael. 1992. "What Librarians Need to Know to Survive in an Age of Technology." *Journal of Education for Library and Information Science* 33, no. 3 (Summer): 226–240.

McGill, Michael E., and John W. Slocum, Jr. 1994. *The Smarter Organization*. New York: John Wiley and Sons, Inc.

Naisbitt, John. 1992. *Megatrends*. New York: Warner Books.

Naisbitt, John, and Patricia Aburdene. 1990. *Magatrends 2000: Ten New Directions for the 1990's*. New York: William Morrow & Co.

Payne, David E., Faye N. Vowell, and Lendley C. Black. 1991. "Assessment Approaches in Evaluation Processes." *NCA Quarterly* 66, no. 2 (Fall): 444–450.

Payne, David E., Faye N. Vowell, and Lendley C. Black. 1992. "Assessing Student Academic Achievement in the Context of the Criteria for Accreditation." *A Col-*

lection of Papers on Self-Study and Institutional Improvement, 1992. Chicago: NCA.

Rush, James E. 1993. "Technology-Driven Resource Sharing." *Bulletin of the American Society for Information Science* (June/July): 19–23.

Seiler, Lauren H. 1992. "The Concept of the Book in the Age of the Digital Electronic Medium." *Library Software Review* (January/February): 19–29.

Senge, Peter. 1990. *The Fifth Discipline: The Art and Practice of the Learning Organization*. New York: Doubleday.

Steele, Colin. 1993. "Millennial Libraries: Management Changes in an Electronic Environment." *The Electronic Library* 11, no. 6: 393–402.

Tapscott, Don, and Art Caston. 1993. *Paradigm Shift: The New Promise of Information Technology*. New York: McGraw-Hill.

Toffler, Alvin. 1980. *The Third Wave*. New York: William Morrow & Co.

Twigg, Carol A. 1994. "Navigating the Transition." *Educom Review* 29, no. 6: 20–24.

Vondran, Raymond F. 1990. "Rethinking Library Education in the Information Age." *Library Education and Employer Expectations*. New York: Haworth Press.

II

Facilities, Services, and Planning in the Revolutionized Environment

6

Reengineering Existing Buildings to Serve the Academic Community

Delmus E. Williams

One of the constant concerns that faces every library every day is the need to provide a sufficient amount of good space to house its collections and service programs. For many years, the concerns of library administrators have focused on the need for enough space to accommodate growing collections. Through the 1960s and early 1970s, most libraries were constantly trying to find funding for new library buildings or library additions, planning them, and/or trying to cope with unforeseen problems at the end of projects. But, while having enough space remains a problem, the focus for most administrations has shifted away from building construction. Financial constraints have made it nearly impossible for many to get new buildings even though there is a significant need to incorporate growing amounts of electronic equipment into library programs. As a result, managers have been required to look carefully at what must be done to adapt existing space to meet changing needs. Many libraries are being called upon to renovate buildings so that they can support technologies that either were not imagined at all or were considered in the realm of science fiction when these facilities were built. This chapter will touch on some of the elements that must be considered as libraries plan to rework their buildings.

THE LIBRARY PROGRAM AND THE BUILDING THAT HOUSES IT

Library programs are being transformed by technologies with a short shelf-life, and the introduction of these devices has had a profound impact on library buildings. In the last five years, new devices for searching optical and electronic databases have been continuously introduced throughout the library. It is likely that these will be either supplemented or replaced by even newer or more powerful equipment over the next five years. At the same time, library users have become increasingly dependent on microcomputers and related equipment in pursuing research. These changes have forever changed the way that library administrators look at library buildings.

Automation in libraries presents two important challenges for the space planner who is being asked to reconfigure space in an existing building to cope with a changing program. The first is that many library facilities now in use were designed to cope with a traditional library program that did not use much equipment and, as a result, do not have the kind of communications, mechanical, electrical, and lighting systems required to support a contemporary program. The second is that these buildings were designed to house programs that changed very slowly. For those who worked in them, accommodating change was defined as coping with collection growth. As David Leroy Michaels noted in 1987, most library buildings have been planned with the expectation that they will serve for 20 to 25 years without major change, and most of the buildings now in use for libraries are older than that (Michaels 1987: 59). It is not unusual to find libraries in buildings that are 50 years old, and it is not unreasonable to expect in the current budgetary climate that many library buildings will be asked to serve for a hundred years or more. These buildings, well constructed and attractive, are often viewed as community or campus landmarks.

But they were designed to deal with paper-based information transfer technologies that have changed little for most of this century. While the concept of what a library is and how it should be equipped has been changing over the last ten years, many library buildings constructed before that have not. They remain little more than attractive warehouses whose designs accommodate storage and quiet reading areas better than they adapt to new technologies. The appropriate metaphor for the classical library, in the words of the authors of the program statement of the new library at Case Western Reserve, is the container, emphasizing "the existence of the physical container of knowledge, the ownership of that container, the housing of the container, and the ordering of that housing in some structure that allows its retrieval" (1992: 2–3). But library programs are moving away from that model. If library buildings are to cope with the unprecedented amount of change that has taken place and continues to occur in our business, they must also change. They must incorporate into this "container" design features that can accommodate the peripherals required to support an information agency that is, in the words of Lawrence Murr and James Williams, "a transparent knowledge network providing 'intelligent' services to business and education through both specialized librarians and information technologies" (Murr and Williams 1987: 7). Relationships must be redefined among library programs; access must be provided to the utilities required to support electronic equipment; and space must be provided for new services required to support library activities.

SPACE NEEDS OF THE MODERN LIBRARY

Change is coming to libraries, and changes must be made in library buildings if they are to cope with the information environment that is bearing down upon them. Every library must now look carefully at the space it occupies with an eye toward carefully balancing aesthetic considerations with the requirements of a program of information delivery that combines the use of traditional paper formats with the use of a wide array of electronic tools.

The building that emerges from this consideration must combine elements that make the library functional in a time of rapid change, and, at the same time, maintain the aesthetic presence of the library as the intellectual center of a community or campus. The building must accommodate new technologies. At the same time, it must recognize that the shift to alternative mechanisms for the delivery of information is not complete. In fact, neither the direction change will take nor its implications on library programs has yet become entirely clear.

The building must also be more accessible in a number of ways. If the planners at Case Western (1992) and many others are correct, the learning process and the information habits of library clients are changing; and the library of the future will require that clients be connected to a wider variety of information resources than any library can hold. Most libraries have already begun to make provision for the computer user who accesses information from home and work. They have also begun to consider the need to provide access to resources that are not housed in the library but can be obtained from other sources on demand. However, it is not clear that the solutions now offered are sufficient to meet demand. It is also clear that libraries have not yet sufficiently considered the needs of users who carry their own equipment wherever they go and who might need to "dock" into the information systems that can support their work. This kind of virtual access to information resources will be increasingly important as notebook computers become as common as three-ring binders among the tools of the researcher.

The building must also accommodate other clients who have not always been served, including patrons with a variety of physical and mental challenges. While the Americans with Disabilities Act does not require existing structures to be modified to meet these people's needs, it specifically states that these patrons be accommodated in any new facility or in any facility where structural changes are made.

Library buildings must also be safe and comfortable for those who staff them and those who use them. When construction projects are undertaken, the contractor must bring the building into conformance with current building codes, and this may entail changes in wiring, fire suppression equipment, plumbing modification, and asbestos removal. Lighting must also be designed to accommodate existing and anticipated programmatic needs, as well as changes that cannot be foreseen. Library planners must also buy ergonomically designed furniture to make workers and users comfortable.

Above all, the library must be flexible. Because of their cost, buildings are necessarily long-term investments with life expectancies, as noted earlier, of twenty years or more (Michaels 1987). The technologies that libraries are now encountering can be expected to be in place for as little as five years. Planning for space needs must take into account what Ottervik and Corallo call the theme of "unknown new technology" (1984: 17). Library space planners must accept the fact that libraries may have to devote either more or less space to house computer equipment that is either more or less distributed throughout the library; must accommodate either more or less support staff in the inner recesses of the library; must allow for either more or less space to cope with growing collections; and must be prepared to support new relationships among library departments, between the library and other providers, and between the library and those who use it.

To cope with the new information age, buildings must be prepared to change. David Bell (Abraham 1983) contends that libraries must be viewed as works in progress and building projects as continua that extend beyond the range of perception. In his view, the building must remain forever incomplete so that it can accommodate change within the context it must support. Decisions must accommodate the understanding that space will change. Libraries must be designed to accommodate those changes. The difficulty is that most buildings that libraries now occupy were not built at a time when that need was understood.

SPACE PLANNING FOR THE LIBRARY

The underlying problem facing modern library managers, both in dealing with facilities and in dealing with changing library programs, is that library organizations and the planning processes they use are designed to deal with incremental change spread out over a decent interval. Libraries have always been conservative organizations. But libraries are now constantly changing in large and small ways and are facing a major paradigm shift that is expected to transform the way they do business altogether. Other chapters deal with the kind of programmatic changes that library administrators are anticipating and the challenges that face the information provider as access to information expands. But suffice it to say that change is coming upon us more quickly than ever before at a time when resources are more limited than they have been at any time in the last twenty years. From a facilities standpoint, this means that the manager must be prepared to adapt a facility that was designed with a different world view in mind (Kapp 1987). If library organizations are to prosper, they must eliminate the moorings that tie them to traditional programs so they can respond more rapidly to change.

To further complicate matters, it is not yet possible for most libraries to talk about eliminating existing programs to accommodate new ones. In a recent article, Michael Gorman (1991) noted that the immediate future of the library program is more likely to be an enhanced version of its present one than something that is radically different. Collections will continue to grow, and, while new formats like the electronic journal and the electronic book will appear, it is not yet clear which of these formats will be permanent and which will remain mere curiosities. It is also not certain which, if any, of the old formats will be superseded or de-emphasized as new technologies are introduced. While most people now see a different model for the delivery of information in the future of all users, there is no real agreement as to whether this will take the form of a complete shift to new media of delivery or merely add to the array of technologies that we now use. As Lawrence Murr and James Williams (1987) noted, this uncertainty means that administrators must recognize that service patterns will change and that the buildings housing library programs must be designed to provide a flexible environment that can accommodate whatever changes occur. But at the same time, the old programs and the obligation to maintain paper collections remain.

In some cases, the need to upgrade support for existing technologies and to incorporate flexibility into the program can be met only through new construction. But in many instances, cost and political considerations will rule out any new building. Renovation will be the only option available. But while renovation will often seem attractive, design considerations incorporated into the building at the time of construction often present a variety of challenges that will complicate the project. If one is to balance the need for an attractive facility and the requirement to enhance its utility, the needs of a traditional library with those of an electronic virtual library, and the needs of the user with those of the staff, careful consideration will have to be given to both what is included in the library before the project begins and what should be included in the facility when construction is completed. The planner will be required to strike a balance between beauty and practicality, while keeping a careful eye on budgetary concerns. At the same time, library managers must carefully consider the effect of any changes on the support the library must have from the community that it serves and on internal organizational considerations.

RENOVATING THE LIBRARY

Thus far this chapter has concentrated on a generic set of problems that will have to be dealt with in any construction project. But what are the special concerns that are likely to confront those charged with modifying an existing structure? In a case study relating to the renovation of the California State Library, Kathy Hudson (1987) gives an example of the kinds of problems that might be encountered in a remodeling project. The Library and Courts Building that houses the library was first occupied in 1928. It consists of a thirteen-tier steel stack tower surrounded by three public rooms, each of which are distinctive examples of the ornate Classical Greek architectural style of the building. Floors are marble, terrazzo, and aggregate flooring that are typically five to nine inches thick, and, in some rooms, covered with mosaics. There are decorated ceilings ranging from eleven to twenty-five feet in height throughout the building. Many of the rooms contain large pillars, some decorative and some load bearing. The interior walls of the building are made of a variety of materials, but all are covered with plaster and complemented with baseboards of wood or marble. Some rooms are decorated with murals.

A facility of this sort, built before telephones were commonplace, before electricity was used for much other than lighting, and before air conditioning, presents a real challenge for the modern librarian. This facility is not designed to support automated library systems. Renovation will have to take into account the aesthetics of a monumental building whose architecture is valued enough to be included on the National Register of Historic Places. At the same time, renovation must adapt the facility to meet the needs of a modern library and develop the kind of flexibility that will be required as the library program develops.

While this is a difficult case, it may not present the extreme. Many buildings built before and somewhat after World War II included core stacks specially reinforced to accommodate book storage. However, these buildings often were not provided with proper floor-loading capacities for the reading rooms surrounding these stacks. They also included solid floors, high ceilings, and monumental adornment to establish the library as a powerful symbol of learning in the community. Many libraries are housed in buildings designed for other uses that have been refitted for library use. In these facilities, cost limitations, and concerns about the best use of space to meet immediate needs, have often taken precedence over accommodating growth and change.

It is common in newer buildings to find that architects have not built in the kind of flexibility required to accommodate the automated systems that are now being incorporated into library programs. Library services and the philosophy that undergirded them changed little between 1920 and 1980, and many library buildings were constructed during that period. This was a time when Library Services and Construction Act funds were readily available and when college campuses were growing. By the late 1980s, when it became clear that library programs would soon be changing in fundamental ways, the buildings were in place, and change had to be made around them. As Case Western planners (1992) noted, the building has produced boundaries, and the renovator must find ways to either accommodate those boundaries or eliminate them.

Few new buildings have been equipped to deal with online catalogs, microcomputers, CD-ROMs, and other devices that are becoming so much a part of the modern library. Perhaps more to the point, even fewer are prepared for the kinds of changes that we can expect in years to come. Until recently, most librarians did not anticipate the value of this technology (nor did anyone else for that matter), or the programmatic changes that would be required to accommodate it. It is no small wonder that architects did not consider them in building programs. As a result, libraries will almost always have a generous amount of space allotted for a card catalog, prominent space close by for technical services, and ample stack bays. They are less likely to have an appropriate capacity for running wire for communications and electrical outlets to allow users to conveniently use laptops, microcomputers, and other workstations.

This is not to say that changes have not been made to update facilities over time, but these may actually complicate the planning process for those charged with renovating the facility. The introduction of various generations of telephones and the rewiring of the electrical system in buildings often means that old cable is left in conduits, making it difficult to understand wiring patterns. While the original plans for the building may clearly note where wire was expected to go, conduit added later is not always as clearly documented. The charting of raceways for newer cable can be a real challenge. The addition of ducts for air conditioning and the upgrade of electrical circuits and plumbing may have made the building more useful over time, but sometimes those charged with adding these "modern" conveniences either cannot or do not take into account the access provided to plumbing and wiring closets in the original plans, making further change more difficult. In situations where the library includes the original structure and wings built later, it is common for additional difficulties to be encountered in trying to run wire between the older and newer structures, heating and cooling the facility uniformly, and developing a coherent plan that efficiently uses all available space.

BEGINNING THE PROJECT

When redesigning a facility, both the building being inherited and the expectation for the structure must be considered. If the building has significant historical interest to the community, every effort should be made to maintain its character both from an aesthetic and a political viewpoint. This might not be easy. Outfitting old buildings with air-conditioning ducts, computer rooms, and electrical closets without changing the exterior of the building limits options and sometimes may appear to waste space. But even when the building is not listed on the National Register of Historic Places like the California State Library, buildings may be governed by rules established by state funding agents or parent organizations that require them to preserve the facade. For instance, the Illinois Secretary of the Interior's "Standards for Rehabilitation" explicitly states that exterior alterations in existing structures will not be tolerated ("Secretary" 1991).

It is also important to realize that a renovation will cost more than expected and yield less than originally anticipated when done. Before a project of this sort can begin to show any real substantive improvement in the building, expensive work is likely to be required to remove asbestos, meet current building codes, and meet the requirements of the Americans with Disabilities Act. It is also likely that stack aisles will have to be widened, limiting shelving capacity, and that traditional desks will have to be replaced with larger ones designed to accommodate electronic equipment. Libraries will likely have to do without space that one might have expected to save through automation. In a survey of California public libraries, Ruth Harder (1995) found that computerized catalogs generally required more space in public areas close to the Reference Desk than did card catalogs, and it is likely that this will continue to be so. Search sessions have become longer as patrons have discovered that they can search the catalog, see if books are available on shelves, search indexes, communicate with reference librarians, order interlibrary loans, and download data into personal bibliographies all from the same workstation. As more patrons become aware of these options and adjust their research strategies to use them fully, the demand for additional workstations will increase.

When all is said and done, renovation may produce a more useful library, but it is likely that the result will be a building that will not be inexpensive, that will use the space better than before but that will still be cramped, and that will represent a compromise between what is really needed and the barriers of the original structure that cannot be overcome.

Library Functions and Functional Relationships

The renovation of the library provides an excellent opportunity for managers to rethink the relationship among library services, the media that they are using to deliver information, and the departments that have been established to support library programs. Too often, libraries either have been forced or have chosen to group electronic media together, sometimes to have access to power, and sometimes because they were not conceptually prepared to integrate new delivery mechanisms into established programs. The refitting of space should provide an opportunity to remedy this. It can provide a wider distribution of terminals and other devices than was previously possible.

Renovation can also be used as a catalyst for other changes in the library program and library operations. Electronic systems change the way services are delivered and the way work is done. They change the way the organization functions. But buildings that were built to accommodate traditional programs configured in a specific way also can dictate how the organization works. When the opportunity arises to change the layout of the library to conform to the functional needs of the program, library administrators can think about how operations will function in the changed environment—the kind of organization that best supports these operations. They can also rethink where various components of the library should be located in the building and how much space should be allotted to each department. Managers should ask whether it makes sense to separate cataloging and acquisitions in an electronic environment, if it is reasonable to take up space on the first floor of the library for technical services, and whether it make sense to separate Interlibrary Loan Services from Circulation Services in the new environment. The manager should also understand that the answers to these and other questions will change over time, requiring additional modifications to the building.

Planning for the renovation of an existing structure must take into account new programmatic needs. The increasing complexity of the information environment is likely to increase the need for user training, and space should be identified for use as a classroom where possible. This space should be wired and equipped to support state-of-the-art instructional methods, both for library use and as a place where this equipment can be demonstrated to other campus users. Support may also be required for more complex programs like the University of Iowa's "Information Arcade," an effort designed to thrust the library into the center of efforts to introduce innovative teaching methods on campus (Lowry 1994). In any case, the planning of a revamped facility should provide some opportunity to explore options for program improvement.

Power and Telecommunications

As one develops a plan for a renovated library, probably the most critical component is the provision of access to power and telecommunications outlets. This may also be the most difficult part of the job. The library of the future will depend heavily on the availability of these two elements, but the kinds and amount of equipment that will be needed is far less predictable (Michaels 1987). As Jay Lucker put it, "If the computer terminal replaces the card catalog, and the CD-ROM replaces the abstract/index table, something is sure to replace both of them!" (1987: 87). It is clear that most libraries do not have sufficient power or sufficient telecommunications capacity to deal with the growth of computer equipment. Most libraries are also finding that their capacity to buy computer terminals is constantly exceeded by the demand for access. In the university environment, it is likely that this demand will be met through the provision of user workstations where patrons can bring equipment into the library, plug in their gear to both phone and electrical lines, and use library systems to access information. While this can be expected to relieve the requirement for constant investments in computer equipment, it will require a very different approach to running cable in the library building.

Accommodating this kind of flexibility in a new building can be expensive, but it is possible using raised flooring and/or dropped ceilings. But these options are not always available in older buildings. Raised flooring is prohibitively expensive in renovations, and dropped ceilings can block architectural adornments that are important to the integrity of the interior design. In newer buildings built on grids bounded by support columns, unobtrusive wiring can be made to follow the contours of the ceiling and then be dropped to the floor either along the columns or in prelaid conduit within the column. This can help, but it limits the number of places that will support terminals to areas close to walls or columns and may not be ideal.

Getting conduit from walls and columns to sites in the middle of the floor is a challenge. Running power and other lines on the floor poses problems. Laying conduit in solid concrete floors is expensive and difficult, and safety and fire regulations often forbid the use of conduit above the floor. A variety of people recommend carpet tiles that will allow the use of flat cabling under carpeting as a possible solution to this problem. This may not protect cabling in high traffic areas and may lead to an unreliable communications network (Kelsey 1987). Terminals can be arrayed in clusters and furniture can be used to hide wiring. But often the only way to get cable to the right places is by running it along the ceiling and then dropping power poles to individual terminals or terminal clusters. However, these are not particularly attractive and can detract from the ambiance of the building.

It is also critical that computers have secure power supplies. Interruptions and spikes in power can damage computing equipment and the files they maintain. Investments made to insure the library has an independent power source that is capable of providing dependable amounts of power and an uninterrupted supply to provide backup are critical. This can limit the potential interruptions.

Cabling a renovated building will always require a certain amount of compromise. The library is unlikely to ever get as many terminals in as many places as necessary in a building that was designed to have none at all. The degree to which the compromise will favor those who are interested in new concepts of service will depend on the limitations of the original structure and the amount of money one is willing to invest.

Lighting

Lighting will always be a source of debate among those who plan library buildings and will cause problems for those who try to renovate them. Old buildings frequently relied wherever possible on natural lighting. Newer ones generally followed David Kaser's (1987) recommendation that the library have uniform lighting throughout the building to enhance its flexibility. However, many planners now feel that lighting should contribute to the ambiance of the building. Natural light and the fluorescent lights used in standard lighting grids can cause glare on computer screens and damage acidic paper.

In many cases, fixed task-lighting is recommended as an appropriate solution, but task-lighting is expensive and can limit the flexibility of the building (Bazillion 1991). The planner cannot anticipate the exact siting for all present and future needs for workstations. Fixed task-lighting will limit the capacity to change the layout to meet programmatic needs. Margaret Beckman (1987) suggests that the best solution might be to provide low ambient lighting throughout the library building and then supplement that with task lighting built into user carrels. However, the capacity to do this may be limited by the ability of the library to get cable to appropriate locations. As a result, many renovated buildings will opt for more natural light provided through properly tinted windows, and for energy-efficient fluorescent lighting with ultraviolet shielding, because these options are less expensive and more attractive (Fisher 1995).

Walls

Walls produce a serious problem for the space planner. Walls serve two purposes. First, many buildings have supporting walls that hold up upper floors and the building's roof. Second, virtually every library uses walls to separate discrete functions within the library. In this way the organization of the library and the program offered are defined in part by the library's walls. Walls constitute boundaries between departments and between people, and when they are viewed as permanent fixtures, they retard the capacity of the organization to change. Where structural walls exist, nothing can be done. But any renovation should avoid the construction of new, full-height walls whenever possible to maintain the flexibility of the structure in the face of changing programmatic needs.

Office landscape systems consisting of floor-to-ceiling demountable wall systems that can be combined with filing cabinets, work surfaces, and book cases can be used to redesign work areas. These provide individual space while maintaining the flexibility of the building. They are more expensive than drywall and do not afford the kind of privacy one might expect from permanent structures. They absorb noise and work especially well in segmenting large work bays (Novak 1987).

Mechanical Systems

Tom Fisher (1995) contends that any mechanical system installed in a building over twenty years ago is outmoded and in need of replacement. While it is no longer clear that modern library systems require the kind of environmental controls that were needed ten years ago, new systems are more energy efficient and are more capable of delivering consistent heating, cooling, and humidity control throughout the facility. In addition, new fire and safety codes require that sprinkler systems and more space for duct work be installed. Specialized filtering systems are also useful in protecting books and other sensitive materials and in making the library a more pleasant and healthful place.

Noise

Whether working primarily with books or with computer terminals, library patrons will always want a quiet place to work. However, the introduction of the computer has made this a bit more difficult. Jay Lucker notes that the space planner should "never underestimate the noise level of a laser printer" (1987: 87). This is increasingly true with other equipment that is becoming part of the library scene. Noise control is a problem that is likely to get worse.

Solutions to the noise problem seem to have common themes. Carpeting,

ceiling tiles or baffled ceilings, and acoustical paneling in individual workstations can help, as can decentralizing user workstations distributed throughout
the facility. When decorated floors or ceilings limit these possibilities, libraries
can establish quiet areas away from the main traffic flows. However, this solution should be used cautiously in that the establishment of "quiet" can lead
to the conclusion that other areas are "loud," which might be counterproductive.
In any case, noise will always present a problem and must be addressed in
planning any library.

Furniture

The use of computers will generally require a workstation that is larger and
more complicated than a traditional library carrel. Michaels recommends that
the traditional 30-by-60-inch desk with a carriage return that is 18 by 36 inches
be replaced by a workstation that is 30 by 66 inches with a carriage return that
is 20 by 42 inches at a minimum. This will accommodate those using a micro-
computer in conjunction with books. Adding a printer requires an even larger
surface. The work surface should be between 28 and 28¼ inches in height for
maximum efficiency and comfort (1987: 62).

New workstations can be expected to be expensive. A systems workstation
with acoustically rated screens, a hang-on shelf, task-lighting, and a work surface
that can accommodate a computer and printer may cost as much as $4,000. A
typical desk may be had for as little as $600 (Michaels 1987: 61)

CONCLUSION

Reengineering an old facility is both an art and a science. The science requires
that planners develop a use plan that copes with the idiosyncrasies of the existing
structure, the vagaries of the law, the opinions of those who work in and those
who use the library, and the needs of the library program. The art is converting
what are often very rigid structures that define programs into what Gloria Novak
(1987) calls "forgiving" buildings, those that will allow managers to redefine
space as the program changes. In a time of rapid change, this kind of facility—
one that will allow the library to absorb new technologies, use them effectively,
add to them as their potential becomes clear, and then discard them for
something else when they either do not prove effective or are made obsolete—
is critical to the success of the library. And in a time when these technologies
will change often, it is likely that reengineering facilities to accept programmatic
change will be required of every manager. The need for these skills will only
increase as the pace of innovation accelerates.

REFERENCES

Abraham, W. V. 1983. "Inheritance and Style: Planning Design at Macquarie Univer-
    sity." *Planning for Higher Education* 11: 1–9.

Bazillion, Richard J., and Sue Scott. 1991. "Building a High-Tech Library in a Period of Austerity." *Canadian Library Journal* 48: 393–397.

Beckman, Margaret. 1987. "The Changing Library Environment: Requisites for Accommodating Change." *Library Hi Tech* 5, no. 20: 89–91.

Case Western Reserve University. 1992. *Kelvin Smith Library, the Electronic Learning Environment Transforming Access to Knowledge: A Program Statement.* Cleveland: Case Western Reserve University.

Dahlgren, Anders C. 1989. "Designing the Flexible Small Library." *Library Hi Tech* 5, no. 20: 78–82.

Fisher, Tom. 1995. "Impact of Computer Technology on Library Expansions." *Library Administration and Management* 9: 31–36.

Gorman, Michael. 1991. "The Academic Library in the Year 2001: Dream or Nightmare or Something in Between." *Journal of Academic Libraries* 17: 4–9.

Harder, E. Ruth. 1995. "Library Automation's Effect on the Interior Design of California Public Libraries." *Advances in Library Administration and Management*, vol. 13. Greenwich, CT: JAI Press.

Hudson, Kathy. 1987. "Historic Buildings and Modern Technology: The California State Library Remodels for Automation—a Case Study." *Library Hi Tech* 5, no. 20: 49–57.

Kapp, David. 1987. "Designing Academic Libraries: Balancing Constancy and Change." *Library Hi Tech* 5, no. 20: 82–85.

Kaser, David. 1987. "Designing New Space: Some New Realities." *Library Hi Tech* 5, no. 20: 87–89.

Kelsey, Donald G. 1987. "Designing Space: Confronting Conflicting Demands." *Library Hi Tech* 5, no. 20: 92–94.

Lowry, Anita. 1994. "The Information Arcade, University of Iowa Libraries." In *Managing Information Technology as a Catalyst of Change: Proceedings of the 1993 CAUSE Annual Conference, December 7–10, San Diego, California.* Boulder, CO: CAUSE.

Lucker, Jay. 1987. "Adapting Libraries to Current and Future Needs." *Library Hi Tech* 5, no. 20: 85–87.

Michaels, David Leroy. 1987. "Technology's Impact on Library Interior Planning." *Library Hi Tech* 5, no. 20: 59–63.

Murr, Lawrence E., and James B. Williams. 1987. "The Roles of the Future Library." *Library Hi Tech* 5, no. 20: 7–21.

Natale, Joe. 1991. "Full and Equal Access: Americans with Disabilities Act." *Illinois Libraries* 73: 599–602.

Novak, Gloria. 1987. "Toward a Forgiving Building: Technical Issues Relevant to New and Existing Libraries." *Library Hi Tech* 5, no. 20: 94–99.

Ottervik, Eric V., and Anthony L. Corallo. 1984. "Integrative Planning for a New Library/Computing Center." *Planning for Higher Education* 12: 15–25.

"The Secretary of the Interior's 'Standards for Rehabilitation.' " 1991. *Illinois Libraries*: 628–629.

7

The Architect's Point of View

Craig Hartman, John Parman,
and Cheryl Parker

INTRODUCTION

Like the written word, works of architecture are a permanent record of our culture, marking our place in history. Since the Renaissance, the library has become inextricably linked with the printed word—and with its accumulation, preservation, and use. Libraries have also grown more common and, in urban and institutional settings, larger and more complex.

Like librarians, architects have been profoundly affected by the explosion of electronic media. The way architects design buildings and communicate information has changed radically in the last few years. Clearly, these changes will continue. The revolutionary promise that the computer has held for architects in the last two decades has only begun to be fulfilled in the last three or four years.

The so-called "electronic revolution" has been around now for almost five decades. The generation of Americans now in their forties has witnessed a remarkable transformation. When they were young, broadcast, network television was just coming into its own, competing with radio and the movies. Computers, which were as ponderous as Mack Trucks in the 1950s and early 1960s, shrank (see Figures 7.1 and 7.2), while telephones developed buttons, went cordless, and finally went cellular and completely portable. Everything has grown smaller, collapsing into everything else or merging across older boundaries. Companies

Figure 7.1. An early Univac computer.

that had nothing to do with each other "got synergy" and are now beginning to create new ways of packaging and moving information and entertainment.

The other dramatic change over this same time period is the astonishing drop in the cost of computing power. Twenty years ago, an IBM mainframe computer, capable of handling 10 million instructions per second, cost $10 million. Later this year, Sony will introduce a video game player, the PCX, which can handle 500 million instructions per second—at a cost of $500. Another company, Microunity, plans a comparably priced "set-top box" for on-demand home video, that can handle one billion instructions per second. By this measure, today's computing power per dollar is two million times greater than it was in the mid-1970s (see Figure 7.3).

Of all the different building types that architects design, it is the library which seems the most directly impacted by this "revolution." The computerization of the library began with the catalog, but has evolved to a point where the books and journals themselves are moving steadily from printed to electronic form. Architecture is a place-making activity, and we are fast approaching the point where it will be necessary to ask if a place called a library is still necessary— just as we might also ask if a book, as a physical object rather than as pixels on a screen, is still useful. Where does the library *as a building* fit in this transformation? Both architects and librarians have a considerable stake in the answer.

Figure 7.2. Timex's Data Link watch—almost the same computing power as a Univac, at a fraction of the size and cost.

THE LIBRARY IN HISTORY

The famous cave paintings at Lascaux in France could be thought of as the first museum or library, or perhaps simply the first publication. The people who painted on those walls had something to say that they wanted to preserve. We don't know how these paintings served them, but what they set down has reached us in a form that connects us to our cultural ancestors in a physical way.

Fortunately, the cave did not survive as the physical model for the libraries that followed, although it may be an ideal setting for our current generation of hackers and net surfers. What is remarkable, though, is how constant the formal qualities of the buildings we call libraries have been over many centuries. From

Product	Year	Performance (instructions per second)	Price
Microunity set-top box	1995	1,000,000,000*	$500*
Sony PCX video game	1995	500,000,000*	$500*
Pentium-chip PC	1994	66,000,000	$3,000
Sun Microsystems 2	1984	1,000,000	$10,000
IBM PC	1981	250,000	$3,000
Digital VAX	1979	1,000,000	$200,000
Cray 1	1976	160,000,000	$20,000,000
IBM Mainframe	1975	10,000,000	$10,000,000

*Estimated

Figure 7.3. The *New York Times'* analysis of how the cost of computer power has fallen in the last twenty years. *Sources:* company reports; the *New York Times*.

the earliest formal libraries through the monastic libraries of the Middle Ages, through the Renaissance and into the 19th century, the nature of the material that was held in libraries and its accessibility to the public changed radically, and yet the casework has probably changed more than the buildings. Like their earlier predecessors, today's libraries still provide space for books—and for the people who read them. They have the same need to accommodate a community of users around the activities of reading and study, and to provide settings that support these activities. An increasing number of modern libraries also serve as archives for special collections of historical value. Skidmore, Owings & Merrill's Beinecke Rare Book Library at Yale University is an example (see Figure 7.4)—and a prototype for more recent libraries that similarly make their special collections an object of architectural as well as scholarly concern.

Another way to look at the history of libraries is to consider their growing accessibility, often in direct response to changes in media no less revolutionary than we are now experiencing. At the time of Michelangelo's Laurentian Library in Florence, the sheer cost of books meant that they had to be chained (see Figure 7.5). Long after Gutenberg and the demise of the chained library, limits to the accessibility of knowledge perpetuated a caste system of an educated elite. When the Transcendentalist Bronson Alcott, father of Louisa May of "Little Women" fame, came into disrepute in Boston with the failure of his Temple School in the early 1830s, the elite of that city persecuted him by withdrawing his privileges at the Athenaeum, a private library that served the well-to-do and, by extension, those whose views they found acceptable. By the end of the 19th century, Andrew Carnegie's successful efforts to build public libraries across America had eliminated this monopoly of knowledge.

Carnegie's philanthropy extended an impulse that could already be seen in the 1830s in the libraries of the Mechanics' Associations. These subscription libraries, founded by what was then an elite, almost professional class of work-

Figure 7.4. Beinecke Rare Book Library at Yale University. Skidmore, Owings & Merrill, architects.

ing men—skilled mechanics and craftsmen and their apprentices—also served as evening schools and forums for social and religious reformers and the nascent labor movement. The Carnegie Library, the prototype for hundreds of public libraries in this country, came to symbolize the right of Americans to free and unhindered access to books as a primary source of knowledge and culture.

In this century, we have seen public libraries proliferate and grow together with their institutional counterpart, the university library, to the point where their need for public funds has begun to exceed the public's willingness to pay—in part because of the growing demand of other cultural institutions for comparable support. As this support has fallen short, libraries have joined museums and symphony, opera, and ballet companies in seeking additional funding from foundations and private sponsors. New urban public libraries continue to be built— Chicago, Phoenix, and San Francisco are three examples. Yet the question must be asked, in this increasingly paperless age, whether it still makes sense to build a library. And if it still does, what kind of building should we construct?

THE ARCHITECTURAL RAMIFICATIONS OF THE NEW MEDIA

The revolution that Gutenberg set in motion 500 years ago—supplanting the chained medieval manuscript with something more portable, affordable, and

Figure 7.5. The chained books of Michelangelo's Laurentian Library in Florence.

available—must have seemed to some of the librarians of that time as a terrible threat to their livelihood: "When they can have books at home, what will become of us?" Albert Dürer's woodcut of Erasmus in his study is emblematic of where things were heading (see Figure 7.6). Yet, as we know, this transformation freed the library from its monastic context and moved it out into the world. There is ample evidence that librarians today are ready to embrace the opportunities afforded by the current revolution in media. Indeed, it is the architects who are nervous, fearing that "virtuality" may eliminate the need for libraries—as buildings—altogether.

Historically, a library was a building organized around two functions—storage and reference. As books and library patrons proliferated, the spatial requirements of these two functions increased and libraries grew larger and larger. Today, the physical connection between storage and reference can be replaced by a virtual one, and the spatial needs of both can be reduced, if necessary, to almost nothing.

Corporate and law libraries, in particular, seem to have moved very far in this direction (see Figure 7.7). With their focus on disseminating information, these libraries can very easily move almost completely online, eliminating the need for a physical setting other than the space occupied by the "cyberians" and their equipment. This trend is reinforced by the increasing number of specialized journals that have shifted to electronic publishing.

Yet even here there is evidence to the contrary. Recently, for example, a

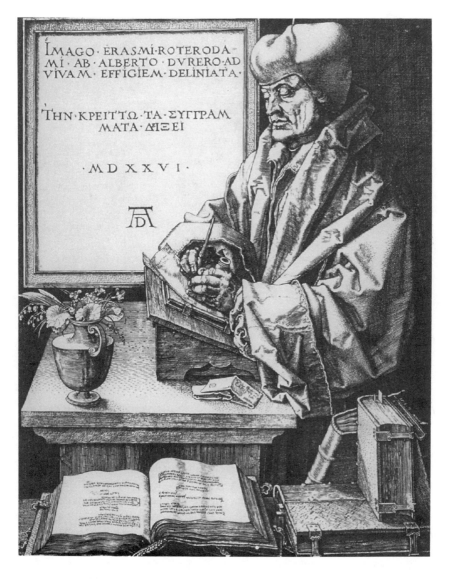

Figure 7.6. Erasmus in his study, as drawn from life by Dürer.

national accounting firm that has used telecommuting to reduce the size of its many offices found that the office library had become the one remaining place where people could meet informally to share their experiences and gain a sense of each other as colleagues and members of the same firm. This characteristic of libraries in general is a crucial one that almost guarantees their perseverance as a building type.

Figure 7.7. The corporate/professional firm library as "communal space." Latham & Watkins Law Firm, Skidmore, Owings & Merrill, architects.

VIRTUALITY AND THE ELECTRONIC REVOLUTION

The electronic revolution, with its promise of virtuality, appeals to our individualism and to our natural desire to save money. If people can access all the information in the world using a computer and a telephone, why do they need libraries at all? The question is comparable to one being posed now in the corporate workplace—is it really necessary to have a "home" for work, or can work actually be done from anywhere, electronic communication substituting for face-to-face contact and the normal settings in which work occurs?

The answer is not simple. The electronic revolution cuts people free of space/time constraints in ways that are liberating and very efficient. It gives them unprecedented access to time-value information, like market quotes, and the ability to sift through and analyze large quantities of information rapidly. This access has a price, however. It requires a substantial investment in equipment, and in gaining the skills necessary to use it to obtain the information. It represents a return, in other words, to the days when access to information was contingent on private, corporate, or institutional sponsorship. The Internet and its commercial equivalents come closest to universal access, but they clearly fall short of the standard set by our public libraries.

From the standpoint of history, the "electronic revolution" is simply the latest chapter in a much longer saga that might be called the "ephemeralization of information." From daubing paint on cave walls, people have evolved through clay tablets, papyrus scrolls, vellum manuscripts, paper, microfilm and microfiche, and finally reached the electronic page, with its promise of paperless, even wireless transmission of ideas and images. Yet the promise of this new technology *is* astonishing. Not only does it offer unprecedented power to access, organize, and analyze large quantities of data, but it has artistic and pedagogical possibilities that are only just beginning to be explored.

THE FUTURE OF LIBRARIES AS A BUILDING TYPE

Where does this leave the library? Will it disappear as a building type? There is some precedent for this in the 20th century—the tuberculosis sanitarium, for example. Libraries may not disappear, but it is not at all clear that they will survive in their present form. John Browning has said of libraries that "instead of fortresses of knowledge, there will be an ocean of information" (1993: 62). Faced with this ocean of information, people may begin to think of libraries as harbors—places where they can find skilled navigators and the latest equipment.

As the need for storage decreases, the service functions of libraries may increase proportionately. Many of these services already exist today, but their importance will increase: teaching, for example, so that people can master the new equipment and information services, new methods of organizing and analyzing data, and new methods of conveying ideas and information; and access to information, so that the "common reader," as Virginia Woolf called her, can have "equality of access" to information, just like her peers in universities, in companies, and in public agencies.

Libraries are cultural institutions, and this aspect of their role will also change. Rather than having to store everything, libraries can now focus their collections and decide where to put their energies. The archival role will become increasingly important, both to preserve historical and cultural material and to serve as a source and guide to this material within the larger network. And as the artistic and pedagogical possibilities of the electronic revolution ripen into new literary forms and learning tools, it is very likely that the library will have a major role in making them accessible to the community at large.

The survival of libraries in the next century—public libraries especially—will depend on their ability to redefine themselves as cultural institutions and as services. As all cultural institutions find themselves competing for limited public and philanthropic funds, we may see the emergence of hybrid institutions—library/museums, for example—that join forces to use them more efficiently. Paris's Centre Pompidou (see Figure 7.8), which combines the functions of a library, a museum, an archive and research center, and a teaching and performance space, is an existing example of this sort of institution.

San Francisco's new Main Library is located in the Civic Center, next to its predecessor. Yet downtown, south of Market Street, there is a new arts district—

Figure 7.8. Centre Pompidou in Paris. Piano and Rogers, architects.

Yerba Buena Center—that brings together museums and performance spaces in an area that is close to the financial center and Union Square and directly adjoins the City's Convention Center. Could the new library have also been located there? Less encumbered by its still-massive storage functions, the answer is "yes." This location might have been a more interesting choice in terms of its proximity and potential synergy with these other institutions.

THE CURRENT STATE OF LIBRARY DESIGN

To understand where libraries as a building type are today and where they are heading, it may be helpful to review some current examples—completed and in design—that show how librarians and their architects are currently thinking about the problem.

The New British Library and the New San Francisco Main Library

Two examples of what might be called "the late 20th century urban public library" are Colin St. John Wilson's New British Library (see Figure 7.9) and the New San Francisco Main Library, designed by James Freed and Cathy Simon (see Figure 7.10). They are best understood as "transitional" buildings that mark the beginnings of change between the "fortress of knowledge" and "ocean of information." Although differing in overall shape and appearance, the two libraries are similar in that each organizes its program around an open

Figure 7.9. The New British Library. Colin St. John Wilson, architects.

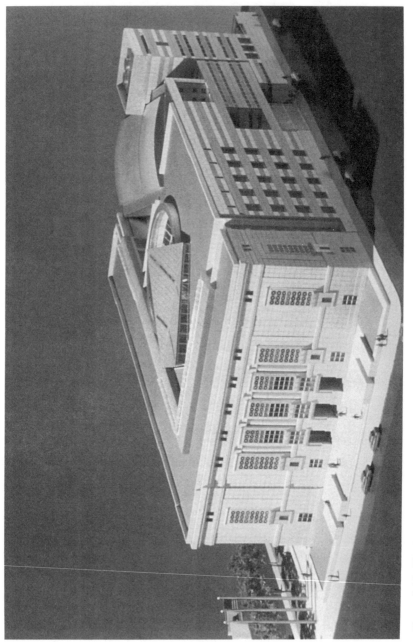

Figure 7.10. The New San Francisco Main Library. Pei Cobb Fried & Partners with Simon Martin-Vegue Winkelstein Moris.

"core"—an atrium or interior plaza. The British Library houses some of England's most famous book and manuscript collections, and the new library is
organized around these collections to the point of making one of them, housed
in a six-story tower, the visual focal point of the building.

While the new British Library more or less turns its modern back on nearby
St. Pancras Railway Station, an icon of late Victorian Gothic Revival, the new
San Francisco Main Library has set itself the more difficult task of trying to
blend in with the city's Beaux Arts Civic Center and the adjoining commercial
district. To accomplish this, the building is designed as two L-shaped blocks—
one in neo-classical style, the other in modern. Although more compact than
the new British Library, San Francisco's new Main Library is similarly organized around an interior core—in this case, an atrium and stairway at the center
of the building—that provides access to its various collections.

These two libraries are "transitional" in that, while they still fulfill a traditional storage function that takes up considerable space, they are primarily dedicated to special collections. San Francisco's Main Library will open with 800
computer terminals and a collection that is largely accessible electronically. The
library reaches out to children and young people, offering them a broad range
of media. It also serves as a resource for historical and informational material
specific to the San Francisco community.

The French National Library

Dominique Perrault's new Library of France in Paris provides yet another
variation on this same organizational scheme (see Figure 7.11). Here, however,
the collections are stored in four towers at the corners of the building, while the
reading rooms and administrative spaces—the *human* spaces—of the library
occupy a low-rise podium surrounding an interior garden. Perrault's radical separation of storage and reference makes it possible to create reading areas that
are open and expansive but at some cost to the building's overall flexibility.

The Teppia Building and Centre National de la Recherche Scientifique

Two buildings which are not libraries *per se,* but possible prototypes for what
libraries could become in the future, are Fumihiko Maki's Teppia Building in
Tokyo (see Figure 7.12) and Jean Nouvel's Centre National de la Recherche
Scientifique (CNRS) Documentation Center in Nancy, France (see Figure 7.13).
Teppia is a product information center, sponsored by manufacturers, with the
information provided on computer and videotape. Despite its elegance, its program already feels outmoded. Like corporate libraries, whose primary function
is to distribute information, Teppia could easily be supplanted by network servers and on-demand video service. Nouvel's CNRS Documentation Center is
more ambitious as described by the architect's statement:

Figure 7.11. The new Library of France, Paris. Dominique Perrault, architect.

What architect would not dream of building the center to be used for the gathering, storing, "transformation," and distribution of knowledge from the four corners of the globe, in every language, in every form, whether mathematical, coded, written, drawn, or photographed. . . . [This is] an information processing factory. Information becomes the raw material. . . . We have satellite dishes, symbols of the worldwide traffic of information; the heliport . . . useful as it will encourage visits from VIPs. Finally, there are the storage facilities, which take up most of the space, forming a massive safe-deposit box for the protection of countless documents. The visitor is left in no doubt that he is in a place where everything is under control, where nothing is left to chance. (Nouvel 1990: 46)

The CNRS facility is centralized for information storage and retrieval. It is another example of a transitional building. By taking on this function at a national level, CNRS relieves other institutions of the need to store and distribute this material. In time, however, the transition of the material itself to electronic form may make this function unnecessary—and the building superfluous. This makes it a questionable model for a library of the future.

The Ruskin Library

The proposed Ruskin Library at Lancaster University in the heart of England's Lake District provides another possible image of the library in the age of the

Figure 7.12. The Teppia Building, Tokyo. Fumihiko Maki, architect.

electronic revolution. Like the new British Library, it uses its collection of rare books and manuscripts as the visual focal point of the building. The architect, Richard MacCormac, has made the building symbolic of Ruskin's aesthetic concerns, drawing on precedents from antiquity as well as from Ruskin's beloved medieval Venice.

John Ruskin was an art critic and social reformer, an outspoken Victorian critic of England's industrial age. How ironic, one might think, that his works have now been issued by Lancaster University on compact discs, and that the library contemplated in his honor will make the fullest possible use of multimedia and electronic access to books, images, and manuscripts. Yet it is likely that Ruskin would not have been as appalled by this revolution as he was by industrialization. He would perhaps look more kindly on technologies that fit so easily into the rural landscape, that allow public access to a unique and vulnerable collection without harming it, and that bring together in one place the functions of a library, a research and teaching center, a museum, and an archive.

The Library of Virginia

The functions described above come together in a new state library and archives building, The Library of Virginia in Richmond (see Figure 7.14). Designed by Craig Hartman of Skidmore, Owings & Merrill, it shares some characteristics of the new British Library and San Francisco Main Library. Yet

Figure 7.13. Centre National de la Recherche Scientifique (CNRS), Nancy, France. Jean Nouvell, architect.

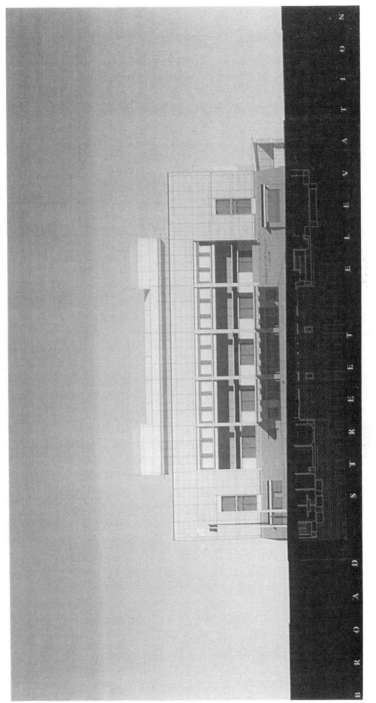

Figure 7.14. The Library of Virginia, Richmond. Skidmore, Owings & Merrill, architects.

its program resembles the Ruskin Library in its effort to broaden the role of the library as a cultural resource and information center for both the Richmond community and the Commonwealth of Virginia as a whole. It fulfills this latter role by serving literally as the hub of a statewide electronic network that links up every public library, down to the smallest branch and village libraries (see Figure 7.15).

The library is located in an area that borders the downtown and civic districts of Richmond. This site is one of eleven in and around Richmond that were considered during initial planning. During this process, there was considerable debate about the merits of a remote, suburban site. Its lower land cost meant that a larger area could be purchased, making future expansion easier. The Building Committee was aware electronic access made this location feasible, yet it was not chosen. There are several reasons for this. The library has traditionally served as the "reference desk" of the Virginia Legislature, and there is a long tradition of "walking over" from the Capitol. It is also a center for genealogical research in the state. Most importantly, however, its large collection of historical documents makes it a cultural resource as important as any museum. Public access to this collection—not only research access, but public access in a museum-like setting—is a major purpose for the building, and one that called for an accessible, downtown location.

Once the downtown site was chosen, the library's potential to contribute to the revitalization of the surrounding area also became a conscious goal for the design. The library fronts on an historic downtown shopping and entertainment street (see Figure 7.16). To fit into this setting and activate it, the design gives street access and visibility to virtually every program element in the library with a public use. The bookstore, auditorium, and conference center, and a substantial public orientation area and museum, are all located at street level and along the perimeter of the building, where visibility and accessibility from the adjoining retail district animate the streetscape (see Figure 7.17). The design also makes provision for a "media wall" along the main shopping street—Broad Street— that is both a means of communication and a billboard—one of the traditional signs of vitality in a commercial district.

The first floor of the library is organized around a central lobby/exhibit space, with its "front door" opening onto Broad Street. At the north end of the lobby, visible from the entry, is a grand stair that leads to the reading rooms and circulation desk on the second floor. All of the public function areas on this level are directly accessible from both the lobby and the street, so they can be used separately by the community at times when the library is closed. These areas are also connected to the statewide electronic network.

The building's separation of its "community" functions from the more traditional ones of the library proper is marked on the exterior by the transition from the rusticated granite base to the *piano nobile* above, which houses the reading rooms that overlook the street.

Functional "layering" is the key to the building's organization above the first

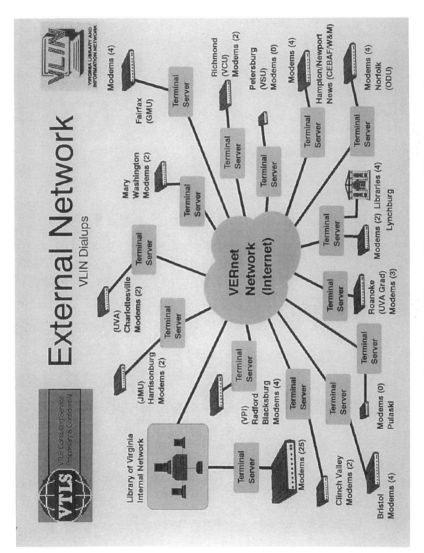

Figure 7.15. The electronic network linking the Library of Virginia to local libraries across the state.

Figure 7.16. Broad Street in downtown Richmond.

Figure 7.17. The Library of Virginia is designed to embrace and activate Broad Street.

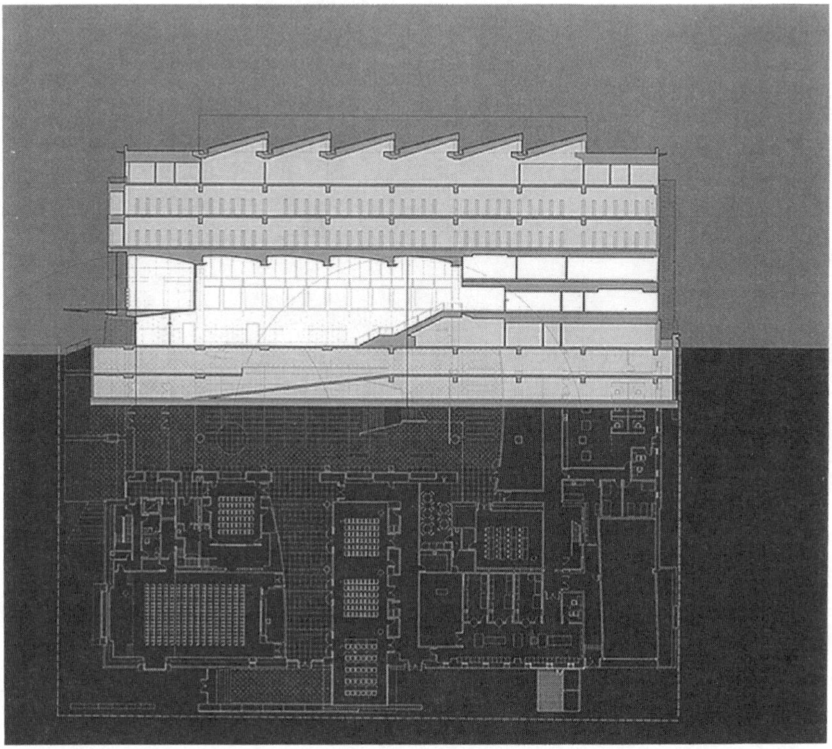

Figure 7.18. Section through the Library of Virginia, showing the clerestories and central public space.

floor. The fifth floor is occupied by administration and technical services—housed in a light-filled loft of north-facing clerestories (see Figure 7.18). The third and fourth floors are allocated to closed stacks, while the second floor and its mezzanine house the reading rooms, reference desk, and rare books. There are two below-grade levels, initially used for parking.

The building adheres consistently to a 30-foot structural bay module. Above grade, this makes for completely interchangeable space, so that stacks and offices, for example, can expand or shrink as necessary to accommodate changes in the library's needs over time. The two below-grade levels are similarly designed for future conversion to book storage—their elevator access and mechanical and structural systems can accommodate this without modification. The library is serviced from four separate cores that carry vertical circulation—stairs and elevators—and provide a "backbone" for the fiberoptics system that carries the statewide electronic network.

The reading rooms—the only single-use areas of the library—are designed for maximum controlled natural light, balanced carefully for reading books or

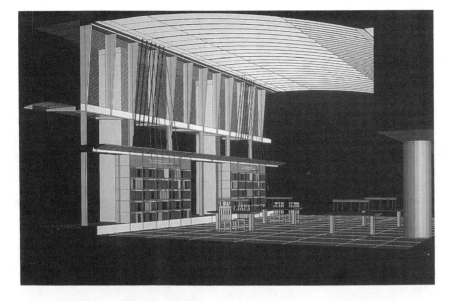

Figure 7.19. Detail of the Library of Virginia reading room showing how daylight is "bounced" into the space.

viewing computer screens. Their reading tables provide plug-in access to the network and to a power source, as well as built-in task lighting. The bookcases in the reading rooms are visible from outside the building, as a traditional symbol of its content (see Figures 7.19 and 7.20).

The library's organization made it possible to reduce cost—something aimed for from the very beginning. The original library program called for 600,000 assignable square feet; the final program is about half that size. The design goes beyond this, however, in consolidating the large volume spaces of the library and limiting their size in relation to the whole. The rest of the building is more like office space to give the desired flexibility. As a result, the library is both compact and straightforward in construction. While it achieves the civic presence expected in this type of building, cost is at the low end of the range—$32 million, or about $73 per square foot (see Figure 7.21).

THE LIBRARY AS A PLACE AND A COMMUNITY

The electronic revolution suggests that the buildings we call libraries may not be necessary much longer. Yet there are still compelling reasons why a library should continue to be a place, and not merely an address on the Internet.

A library today is, almost invariably, a community of men and women with specific training in research methods and information systems. It is also a community that values knowledge and culture and is prepared to instill that value

Figure 7.20. Detail of the Library of Virginia exterior window wall at the reading rooms.

in others. Like any community, it needs a physical setting to give it identity and support its activities and services. The electronic revolution only makes human encounter, which is the real basis of community, more valuable and necessary— not less so. As communities that we now take for granted, like the workplace, lose their status as a given in our society, others—the library among them— will grow in importance.

As libraries free themselves from the need to accumulate and store books and journals, it will be easier to focus collections and begin to find room for other things—training, certainly, and perhaps even allowing writers, teachers, and others in the community to pursue research and creative work independently. This is in keeping with the library's historic role in providing public access to culture and information—the legacy of Carnegie and many others.

The library of the future has to be more flexible than the library of the past— as easy and inexpensive to change as an office building. It also needs to be capable of more intensive use, for we live in an era when we can no longer afford buildings that are not used to their fullest capacity. To accomplish this, libraries may have to share facilities with other institutions and users. The result of this merger could be something richer and more interesting than a single use facility.

Figure 7.21. Model view of the Library of Virginia.

The challenge is considerable, both for librarians and their architects, but there is no reason to doubt we will both rise to the occasion. Nor should we doubt that there will *be* an occasion—libraries are still important and necessary, and we can expect to be building them well into the next millennium.

REFERENCES

Browning, John. 1993. "Libraries without Walls for Books without Pages." *Wired* 1: 62.

Nouvel, Jean. 1990. "Centre National de la Recherche Scientifique (CNRS) Documentation Center." *GA Document* 27: 46.

8

Collection Development in the Revolutionized Environment

Johannah Sherrer

The need to deal with issues associated with electronic data, publications, and processes permeates every level of librarianship in every size and type of library. Technology that was once the purview of the elite is fast becoming a reality for all librarians. For the most part, the impact of technology on libraries has centered on processes. Librarians eagerly embrace technology that makes what is currently done easier and faster. The automation of library processes and the continual refinement of procedures and techniques is now common place. Without quite realizing it, librarians choose, evaluate, and purchase automated systems costing hundreds of thousands of dollars with more confidence and assurance than in preceding years. Technical terms, foreign to many only a short while ago, are now commonplace.

The technological revolution presents library management with opportunities to enhance collection development activities. In the areas of cataloging and acquisitions, faster processing options are continuing to evolve in terms of rapid record searching, electronic ordering, check-in, claiming and cataloging. Libraries are demanding and receiving speedier approval plans and prepublication announcements, and improved international purchasing procedures. It is now time, however, to move beyond how library systems acquire and process materials and begin integrating electronic sources and materials into our collections and services. It is time to stop thinking of our collections in terms of print sources and ownership even though these types of sources predominate our collections. It is imperative that libraries move the electronic environment even deeper into collection development activities. It is time to coordinate the impact of access on daily resource management decisions and move beyond access to effective document delivery. More importantly, it is time to bring institutional collection decisions out of the parochial realm and into the wider context of information and materials availability at large.

This chapter will address a redefinition of collection development in the electronic environment, discuss new spins on selection and weeding decisions in an electronic environment, challenge the assumptions of a core collection, appraise existing resource-sharing options, and discuss the radical changes needed to move collection development into the next generation of activities, and conclude with real time strategies for building and managing collections in an electronic environment.

A NEW DEFINITION FOR COLLECTION DEVELOPMENT

The invention of the printing press revolutionized society because of the way it altered communication. Communication patterns were extended, ideas spread more rapidly, and it became easier to record and save knowledge/information. It marked the growth of vast private libraries developed primarily by and for individuals. Just as surely, today's technology is radically changing communication patterns, the speed of communication, and the process of recording, saving, and transmitting information. Anyone who believes that developments in information technology still mean business as usual for libraries is vastly mistaken. It is imperative that libraries rethink collection development activities in the light of this expanding technology. It is a mistake to believe that the foundation of collection development is as it has always been and that it lacks only the incorporation of electronic sources into existing collections.

Daily collection development decisions are profoundly influenced by the electronic environment. Technology is adding new dimensions to collection building with each advance in communications development, and libraries continue to wrestle with the vast implications of information dissemination in the electronic world. There is a tendency for many to avoid or eliminate from consideration anything that falls outside a perceived budgetary reality. While an effective way to limit information to a manageable reality, this operational methodology is not valid in the electronic environment. Libraries will continue to add materials in all formats to their physical collections, but of *equal* importance is what does not reside in-house. If libraries fail to incorporate responsibility for management of information residing outside of what is purchased, or leased, or subscribed to, they can and will be replaced by commercial document delivery vendors or private information brokers. Libraries that fail to incorporate information facilitation into collection management activities will fail to fully develop their collections in a coordinated, logical fashion. The very foundation of collection development needs to be refocused to include information dissemination and information accessibility as central to most decisions in collection activities. Resources that can be provided on-demand or information that is fee-based in a manner similar to "pay for view" need to be incorporated into the overall development of collections.

The process of formally redefining an activity or process can serve to help refocus thinking on a particular activity. One way to change direction is to redefine the activity in a manner that eliminates or de-emphasizes former priorities. In terms of collection development, a redefinition means a formal, recognized movement away from in-house print-based materials and an expansion of the concept to include sources not owned.

The following is an example of a goal and subsequent definition that attempts to refocus collection activities in an electronic environment. It is designed to fit a college library but it can be adapted so that the key ideas apply to either public or research libraries.

Goal

The Library Resource Development Goal is to *maximize* ready access to information resources, which support the curriculum and research needs of the college, organizing them in a manner which invites use and utilizes networking capabilities to link resources to any authorized user.

Definition of Resource Development

Resource development refers to the activities involved in identifying, evaluating, and making available monographs, serials, and other information resources which support the curriculum of the college, in print, electronic, microform, or media format. Effective resource development requires consistent and regular interaction with the students and teaching faculty based on a mutual understanding of the aims and goals of resource development.

Resource Development Responsibilities

Resource development responsibilities for librarians in this model could include:

- To be aware of information and materials relating to a field of study whether or not owned by the library.
- To identify, evaluate, and select for purchase appropriate materials for college acquisition as they relate to the curriculum.
- To identify, select, and evaluate materials currently residing in the public domain or available through the Internet.
- To manage and shape the collection in concert with the faculty, students, and curriculum of the college.
- To integrate materials of all formats into a balanced and representative collection that will support the curriculum of the college.

Implicit in this definition is a far more pronounced link between the user of today as opposed to the user of tomorrow. Research libraries pride themselves and their collections on the ability to serve future clients and to anticipate their needs. The underlying assumption is that current client needs are automatically being met because of collection decisions made in previous years. Reference librarians are the primary agents for assisting users in locating previously acquired items. Now, however, reference and collection development are so closely related that continuing to maintain separate staffs for the two functions is questionable. It is questionable not only because of the numbers of staff required to maintain two units but also because of the ability of such a system to actually serve and meet patron needs. The electronic environment is forcing all libraries to deal with immediate patron needs as a first priority. The electronic environment is forcing bibliographers to deal with availability of materials to meet existing patron needs. It is forcing reference librarians away from pure bibliographic sources and into the document itself.

In pre-electronic days, the assumption in small libraries was that limited budgets forced the collections to serve immediate needs as defined by curricula for college libraries and by community needs for public libraries. Staffs in small libraries were often frustrated by the knowledge of a source existing beyond their budgetary grasp. Efforts to continually refine the collection in order to meet *collective* user needs were the norm. In the electronic era, however, small libraries can have access to information and resources on a one-time basis to satisfy individual user needs. Small libraries can now afford to address the specific information needs of their users.

NEW ASPECTS OF DECISION MAKING IN COLLECTION DEVELOPMENT

Does this mean that in the electronic environment libraries will orient services, including collections, to working with individual users rather than the collective needs of the community? Or put another way, is technology making it possible to justify meeting one client's need over the primary goal of the general collection development efforts? Should it? Is it possible that libraries have been working so long to meet only the commonly held needs of clients that the opportunity to meet specific needs is foreign or maybe wasteful? Are libraries so preoccupied with providing equal service that they are jeopardizing the opportunity to meet exact patron needs?

Conceptual Reevaluation

Technology is doing far more than simply causing libraries to add electronic texts and bibliographic access points. It is causing the profession to reevaluate the underlying assumptions on how—and from whom or where—we acquire information, how it is distributed, who receives it, and the delivery method used. Library collections and services in the electronic environment can meet exact user needs more effectively than ever before if they move beyond regarding the physical collection as the primary collection. But in order to do this, all collection-building efforts need to be guided by the implications that electronic resources are bringing to the collection as a whole. Each purchase decision, including print titles, will be affected by emerging technologies. Libraries that are seriously engaged in rethinking all collection management issues must be able to recognize the impact of communications development on the most elementary of collection decisions. Hiring "experts" to incorporate electronic sources while maintaining separately developed print collections is not an effective solution in any size library.

In the pre-electronic era, it was possible to develop collections in isolation from other library decisions or library functions. Hierarchical management structures, physical locations of offices, and the ideology that attempted to develop complete collections, allowed collections to grow regardless of current use patterns. A pre-electronic environment mind-set is characterized in college libraries as efforts to show planned development in collections. These are predominately efforts to match titles with curricula, course syllabi, or *Books for College Libraries*. In public libraries it is characterized by concerted efforts to match acquired titles to community programs, needs, and preferences. In each case, the majority of acquisition funds are used to acquire materials in anticipation of specific needs. However, when existing collections fail to meet individual patron queries, one of two things usually happens: Either collection decisions are reconsidered for the future while the particular request goes unmet, or the patron is referred to the uncertain outcomes of interlibrary loan.

NEW CONSIDERATIONS

In the post-electronic era new considerations must be addressed, especially if librarians accept the theory that the physical collection is not primary. First, selection expertise must be developed across formats. This means that not only traditional print and microformats must be considered but also a variety of electronic formats as well. These include bibliographic files, full-text numeric files, multimedia, and application software. Second, the opportunity to pay for access as needed should be a routine part of the decision tree used in materials selection. Third, decisions regarding how resources are presented to the public are more significant than ever in the electronic realm. For instance, does it do any good for staff to know that the full text of a serial title is available through Dialog if that fact is not readily apparent to the public? Decisions to rely on vendors for on-demand material must be apparent to users. Fourth, key selection decisions now include whether or not a resource will appear on the campuswide network, the library LAN, and the stand-alone workstation, and what has print backup, micro backup, CD-ROM backup, or no backup at all. Fifth, archival decisions regarding the permanency of the item to the collection need considerable revamping in all libraries. Do libraries need to retain archival collections of electronic data and text in each location, or should libraries work toward a national model with end-user retrieval capabilities? Should libraries be working toward regional solutions? Sixth, resource decisions now require a minimum understanding of hardware and software issues to effectively build in an area. The current plan in many libraries is to hire "experts" to deal with the electronic implication of materials and to develop the print collections separately. The thought processes of these two activities cannot remain divided if collection work is to proceed in a coordinated manner.

ORGANIZATIONAL MODELS FOR COLLECTION DEVELOPMENT IN THE ELECTRONIC ENVIRONMENT

Where does one begin? There are no rules or standards in this domain yet. Few rules of thumb exist, and there are no assurances that when a course of action is selected, it won't be quickly outdated, enhanced, or replaced by something touted as better. In spite of this, sitting back and waiting for a course of action to be developed by someone else is an error far more serious than inaction. One good rule of thumb is to let patron use guide decision making. Collection should be developed with the needs of existing patrons as primary, especially in terms of technological applications.

Libraries having a large staff are referred to an article by Samuel Demas, titled "Collection Development for the Electronic Library: A Conceptual and Organizational Model" (1994: 71-80). Demas's article addresses the implications of electronic publishing on collection development decision making, particularly in selection decisions. He stresses that it is essential for librarians to develop expertise across formats. While that is developing, however, he sets forth a model for research libraries that will enable them to make selection decisions in group settings that involve other library units and administrators. It will surely appeal to libraries and to librarians that value process.

In smaller work settings, the issues that Demas outlines are still relevant, but modifications to his model will allow a speedier and less complex mode of decision making. Smaller libraries face the same issues and decisions as larger libraries, but the opportunity to move at a faster pace, to be more experimental, and to operate in a less structured environment work to their advantage.

STAFFING COMPETENCIES

The electronic revolution is demanding that library collection development staff incorporate the following skills and abilities into their basic competencies.

• Staff must develop selection expertise across formats.

• The ability to course-correct will become increasingly significant in the development of proactive and meaningful collection decisions.

- The ability to understand how users seek and use information in an electronic environment is as essential as subject or discipline knowledge. Each collection decision should start with the user.
- General expertise and the ability to work across disciplines and formats are essential skills in current collection activities.
- Rapid, yet judicial, decision-making skills are crucial to moving collection management activities forward.
- The ability to work collaboratively will over-ride specific personal expertise.
- The ability to anticipate and envision a changing world of information exchange and documentation and to develop comfort with subsequent changes is critical.

To thrive and progress in this new electronic world, collections staff should be provided with the following necessities:

- A networked personal computer and access to a printer.
- An e-mail account.
- Internet access.
- Training opportunities in emerging technologies.

By the same token, staff will need to:

- Effectively integrate modern communication technology into daily work processes.
- Demonstrate knowledge of FTP (file transfer protocols).
- Demonstrate knowledge of multimedia products, electronic journals, and discussion lists in their fields and be capable of evaluating such products and formats.
- Demonstrate comfort with information in all formats.
- Demonstrate an understanding of the potential of digital text storage and retrieval.

CORE COLLECTIONS

The electronic environment should be reshaping traditionally held assumptions such as the development of core collections. The development of core collections is the linchpin of collection development in academic libraries, especially college libraries. Studies (Larry Hardesty and Collette Mak 1994: 362-371) now show that the effort has been, for the most part, futile. Hardesty and Mak chronicle the history of core list development and report on a number of overlapping studies, including their own. They effectively demonstrate that more than 50 years of effort have failed to produce core collections in libraries. Apparently, the only real overlap is in intent and definition. Overlap title studies, as reported by Hardesty and Mak, show a remarkably small overlap in practice.

The concept of "core collections" is based on several assumptions. One is that undergraduate library collections should be significantly different than research library collections. For a while it was standard practice at large research institutions to build, staff, and maintain separate library facilities for undergraduates. The basic justification was that undergraduates could succeed quite well with a core collection that matched the core curriculum. In theory, idealistic definitions and rationale were developed that directed academic librarians to pursue the development of the "core collection." Hardesty and Mak artfully delineate the evolving definitions of a "core collection." In the 1930s the contributors to *A List of Books for College Libraries* were advised to limit their recommendations to titles "regarded as essential or highly desirable for the proper conduct of undergraduate teaching" (Hardesty and Mak 1994: 362). In the 1960s, *Books for College Libraries* (*BCL*) based the selection of items included on the premise "that there is a body of knowledge—the classics, the important scholarly titles, and the definitive works on all subjects of interest to any undergraduate community—which should be in any college library" (Hardesty and Mak 1994: 363). The most recent *BCL* (1988) still aims to provide exact titles for the basic core collection. Hardesty and Mak balance this aim with Thomas Nisonger's advice. Nisonger (1992) defines a core collection as those titles that libraries would wish to hold. Technology allows academic libraries to test efforts to collect a common core of materials. Hardesty and Mak demonstrate effectively that this has not happened. Surprisingly, though, they recommend that the goal is still worthwhile and that academic librarians continue to pursue the development of the "core collection."

Why? Why continue to work toward an ideal that has eluded us for over 50 years? Why is a goal predicated on print publishing standards worthy of continued support? What is the point of developing similar collections when all of our efforts should be directed to acquiring unique sources for collaborative use? Why recommend the building of in-house collections with the right hand when the left hand is bringing the universe of searching to users in every type and size of library. The only valid way to continue thinking about the "core collection" referred to in Hardesty and Mak's article is on a regional or national basis. It is time to challenge the necessity of building a local core collection that is title based. If the theory is correct, these are the titles that need to be digitized first and placed in a National Electronic Library. Local efforts to seek on-site core collection based on a standard such as *BCL* are not productive.

RESOURCE SHARING

As libraries relinquish more and more control to users, it will be their decisions that govern use and the requesting of titles not on-site. In the pre-electronic era, users were basically forced to select from the titles in the buildings' collection. Card catalogs, and early versions of online catalogs, were limited to materials acquired and housed within the institution. In the post-electronic era, online catalogs provide access to titles held outside the home institution, and increasingly, outside the geographic region. In Ohio and Oregon, for instance, users have the choice to search a union catalog over local holdings with the ease of a key stroke. Libraries that offer FirstSearch's WorldCat to users are exposing their patrons to choices from among 31 million records! This kind of global searching is replacing the locally managed primary book collection. FirstSearch's WorldCat use is proof of this. We have known for some time that users eagerly embrace searching remote catalogs through "telneting" and "interneting." FirstSearch makes this very easy to do through WorldCat, and statistics proving its dramatic use over the other databases demonstrate unmistakable evidence of user preference for searching global databases.

Resource sharing is now an absolutely critical function and a pre-eminent user demand. The effort so far by The Online Computer Library Center's (OCLC's) Interlibrary Loan Subsystem has been tailored far too much to the old, outmoded interlibrary loan protocols. It is time to abandon these protocols and reinvent the Interlibrary Loan Subsystem from an end-user perspective rather than the protocol-based, traditional library system. Systems like OhioLink and the proposed Orbis (Oregon Link) are developing effective user-driven interlibrary loan options. Collaborative or complementary resource-sharing services between consortiums and the major bibliographic utilities will allow a powerful national resource-sharing network to be put in place. Linking systems is just the first step in resource collaboration.

It is time to bring resource sharing front and center in collection development activities. Previous efforts at resource sharing can be defined mainly in terms of interlibrary loan and the infamous manual that has guided interlibrary loan departments for years. This manual is procedurally based and predicated on the assumption that from time to time items owned by one library can be lent to another. It was designed as a backup method for getting documents to clients in another library. Most of the procedures are designed to save staff time rather than the users' time. It is understood that interlibrary loan is a favor being performed by one library for another. Often libraries, whether meaning to or not, convey to users that interlibrary loan is the exception rather than the rule. Too often, librarians expect users to be satisfied with access as it is currently offered. In fact, librarians expect users to be satisfied with the collection as it exists. Statistics cited by the Association of Research Libraries (Baker and Jackson 1993) demonstrate that users are increasingly unwilling to limit their scope to prescribed library policies. So while librarians are usually grateful for any kind of service from other libraries, library users expect it as a standard service, not a favor.

Existing interlibrary loan protocols and interaction are usually directed from one interlibrary loan department to another. Interlibrary lending emphasizes cost savings over the speed of service to the user so that we go to "free" or reciprocal agreements first. When speed is a value to the user, it is a "rush" job rather than the norm. Systems that connect the user to the citation and then connect the citation to the delivery of the text will become the standard in user-driven document delivery systems. Most interlibrary loan librarians are more likely to be meeting with their counterparts at other libraries than with their local collection builders or public service librarians. Interlibrary loan is often neglected as a library priority. Within the departments themselves more emphasis is put on borrowing than lending. But in spite of this, or maybe because of it, interlibrary loan is one of the few library activities, other than cataloging, that truly aims to be collaborative outside of the parochial endeavors of the home institution.

The Association of Research Libraries (Baker and Jackson 1993) cites statistics that reflect national trends in interlibrary loan activity. The report states that between 1981 and 1992 lending by ARL libraries grew by 52 percent, and borrowing grew by 108 percent in the nation's largest libraries. When research libraries find themselves increasingly unable to provide sources on-site, the issue is clearly one of a universal context. The report states that although the materials budgets in ARL libraries increased by 244 percent since 1981, their collections grew by only 12 percent. More recent figures indicate that staffing in ARL interlibrary loan units increased by less than 15 percent in the last five years while traffic rose by 45 percent.

Interlibrary loan can no longer be considered a backup mechanism for existing collection failures. The function is now as essential as any library service and needs to be funded in a manner that corresponds to collection development decisions and user needs. In addition, the interlibrary loan function needs to be reassessed conceptually to make it more user-based than rule-based and more user-oriented than personnel-oriented. Library administrators need to look hard at their existing interlibrary loan departments and the role the library is now playing in the delivery of information and services. It is only logical that every library decision that promotes bibliographic access must also promote the library's ability to secure materials not owned.

Users have a different set of expectations for electronic indexes than for the old print indexes. This set of expectations is centered on document delivery with the users in control of the selection of citations. Users will not tolerate or support a library system that fails to incorporate a document delivery system for items not on-site. Special libraries have pioneered this service and academic libraries are beginning to reevaluate their role in the delivery of off-site services. But public libraries lag far behind. The ability of public libraries to successfully incorporate document delivery will be critical to their role as major players in their communities.

Experience with FirstSearch indicates that users prefer searching the universe of information as opposed to local collections. The implications that this has for collection development is vastly important to the success of individual libraries in serving their constituents. To the user, all libraries should be available to anyone who needs to use them. Those of us in private colleges and special libraries know this from the disappointed voices and faces of those who have come in search of our collections and services over many years past. In spite of restrictions and service limitations, access expectations of users show little sign of diminishing. If anything, users' expectations are rising in the electronic environment, not diminishing. Most users think of libraries in a more generic sense, without user restrictions or content limitations. Information, in its many definitions and forms, when made available through libraries, carries with it a set of service expectations not faced by commercial information vendors. The role of libraries as service providers is to facilitate access on the users' terms.

As collection builders, librarians need to work with the major bibliographic utilities to rethink resource sharing in an age of electronic access. Libraries need to move *beyond* access as the identification of what is available to actually providing the information, book, or article being pursued. In short, we need to reconceptualize resource sharing and regard it as a service as vital and as basic as local circulation services.

We cannot adopt and promote a global resource like FirstSearch if we fail to adopt a global view regarding information, its availability, and its dissemination. We must carefully review existing collection practices and determine whether or not they are still relevant. Most important of all, libraries must begin collaborating with the major bibliographic utilities to pioneer a whole new mechanism for resource sharing, one that works with existing regions or groups of libraries in improving the speed and simplicity of interlibrary borrowing.

COOPERATIVE COLLECTION DEVELOPMENT

Cooperative collection development is meaningless unless it is securely and emphatically tied to effective document delivery. So while collection development librarians are documenting the intellectual decisions for cooperative collection development, equal effort must be placed on the policies and procedures that will make these cooperative efforts meaningful. Technology can make document delivery faster if it is a budgetary priority and if there is a firm commitment to acquiring the hardware necessary to project the service to its full potential. The cooperative efforts in place are defined primarily by print collections, and they are motivated by economic circumstances. Library groups almost always start with serial cancellations rather than serial additions; they identify titles not to be kept instead of titles to be maintained and shared. They often ignore, for instance, opportunities for collaborative approval plans for book acquisitions. Collaborative efforts are characterized more as agreements of intent rather than operational to insure the reality of the end goal.

The following elements need to be in place for cooperative resource development to become an operational reality.

- Delivery mechanisms for sharing resources must be user driven.
- Document delivery options must be based on user preferences.
- Collaborating institutions must agree to exact turn-around parameters based on user expectations.
- Ideally, shared collections should share a single user interface.
- Philosophically, cooperative collection development cannot be a second priority.
- It will be beneficial for collaborative endeavors to seek links to a national system.
- State-of-the-art technology must be employed to insure delivery and access.

- Central storage facilities will assist in local preservation and archival efforts.
- Successful cooperative agreements will be those that share as widely and openly as possible. Sidebar agreements opening only portions of a collection to outside borrowers will be time consuming to enforce and difficult to explain to users.

CONCLUSION

The following is a list of specific actions that should be happening in every library as a result of the electronic revolution. Libraries that are not experiencing these events should examine "why not" and libraries that are experiencing these events should be evaluating and reflecting on their outcomes.

- Print reference collections should be physically shrinking.
- Cancellation of print indexes and abstracts should be routine.
- Interlibrary loan traffic should be increasingly accompanied by corresponding increases in staff and budgets for commercial document delivery services.
- Every advance in public accessible databases should be accompanied by a corresponding increase in funds for document delivery.
- Hardware maintenance and repair should be a solid item in every annual budget.
- The development of serial collections should be based on electronic availability.
- Every library should have some type of full-text access and subscriptions to electronic journals and/or list services.
- Most of the above should be happening due to budgetary reallocations rather than a special influx of funds.
- Electronic expansion should be involving networks and collaborative endeavors with other institutions or libraries.
- Most decisions involving electronic products, processes, or data transfer are irrevocably linked to outside partners, vendors, or agencies.

The interaction of emerging technologies and collection development issues is producing an environment that is challenging old assumptions and bringing forward as many questions as it does solutions to problems. Library staff involved in collection assessments and development are finding that technology is fast becoming a factor in every collection development decision, as are the issues of access and document delivery. The electronic environment is diminishing the significance of the size of library collections. It is causing collaborative collection development efforts to affect all libraries whether or not they participate in such endeavors. Emerging technologies are enhancing and encouraging interdisciplinary studies; scholarly communication and general information sources are developing routes without print documentation; and all libraries, including public libraries, are being forced to expand their role in information and document retrieval. All of these factors mandate that each selector carefully reevaluate the basic premise of collections and the appropriate direction of their own efforts. In the final analysis it will be the daily operational decisions of selectors that will reshape library collections in the electronic environment.

REFERENCES

Baker, Shirley, and Mary Jackson. 1993. *Maximizing Access, Minimizing Cost: A First Step Toward the Information Access Future.* Washington DC: Association of Research Libraries.

Demas, Samuel. 1994. "Collection Development for the Electronic Library: A Conceptual and Organizational Model." *Library Hi Tech* 47: 71–80.

Hardesty, Larry, and Collette Mak. 1994. "Searching for the Holy Grail: A Core Collection for Undergraduate Libraries." *The Journal of Academic Librarianship* 19: 362–371.

Nisonger, Thomas. 1992. *Collection Evaluation in Academic Libraries.* Englewood, CO: Libraries Unlimited.

9

Public Services in the Revolutionized Environment

David F. Kohl

In today's fragmented and frantic world, the stately images of the medieval period are not only evocative but reassuring in their stability and timeless grace. For Western culture particularly, the image of the walled monastery, such as the sea-protected Mont Saint Michel in Chartres, France, has an ethereal power as the sanctuary of learning and the preserve of the written record during the regression of culture during the dark ages in Europe. Similarly, isolated fortresses sheltered the classical beginnings of Western culture and provided the seeds for its rebirth in the European Renaissance. That image of the walled repository of learning as an island sanctuary preserving the human record echoes down the centuries and lives on today in our celebration of the great libraries and collections of our time. Just as the medieval monasteries played their role and then faded from the scene, so must our image of and commitment to the great individual library.

The emerging reality is not one of individual, great traditional libraries—a Widner or a University of Illinois—but a mosaic of libraries and collections joined through a transparent web of automation, delivery services, and cooperative agreements. The local library, rather than being the primary collection of resources and services for its patrons, becomes the portal to the larger virtual library and a key building block of a larger, virtual entity.

Public services staff, while clearly not the only individuals responsible for transforming the library, are nevertheless key players in this necessary and important enterprise. Relying heavily on the examples I know best, OhioLINK and the University of Cincinnati (UC), I would like to illustrate the transformation of public service roles and self-understanding in the creation of the virtual library.

Consisting of 41 Ohio-based university, college, and community college libraries, OhioLINK provides the state's academic community with access to 20 million book volumes within 48 hours; online access to 6,000 full-text journal articles; 24-hour-per-day access to a wide range of online reference tools including UMI Proquest, the Wilson Databases, Medline, and library catalogs; use of full-text databases such as Chadwyck Healy's British Poetry and Verse Drama resources; and sophisticated access to the Internet through a subject-based Gopher.

Given the changes and directions of movement to date, there are at least three major themes running through the transformation of public services. The first is a redefinition of library cooperation from the traditional form at the periphery of independent institutions to a much more radical version of cooperation, cooperation at the core.

COOPERATION AT THE CORE

Although librarians as a profession and libraries as organizations have always prided themselves on their ability to cooperate with each other, that cooperation has traditionally been limited. Libraries within a small geographic region generally promote reciprocal borrowing policies. Nationally, interlibrary loan programs have allowed libraries to access materials on a much broader scale. As important as these and similar efforts have been, reciprocal borrowing agreements have often proven fragile, especially when the economy gets tight or the bond levy fails.

The underlying reality is that libraries have always been consistently identified with their collections, the nature of which have been developed to meet local needs. For over two millennia, materials were made available to patrons primarily by collecting them locally. In this paper-based environment, interlibrary cooperation was difficult at best. As in the current environment, two key problems had to be addressed to provide a requested item through the interlibrary cooperative process: confirming bibliographic identity and determining location. Paper-based tools were not adequate. They were by definition out-of-date as soon as they were published. They were incapable of being corrected except by issuing new volumes and were so expensive that only a minuscule portion of the nation's bibliographic holdings were reported. Using a collection in any serious way meant going to that collection. Cooperation was necessarily marginal and limited.

The electronic environment, coupled with financial constraints, has revolutionized interlibrary cooperation. The electronic revolution has matured to the point of providing bibliographic and circulation information to patrons anywhere. An item found in today's electronic library catalog is identified bibliographically and in terms of location and circulation status. In the case of Ohio, for example, this electronic environment has transformed 41 local libraries into a single virtual library of over 20 million volumes.

Rather profoundly, this large and rich collection requires an acceleration of integration. For an OhioLINK library, the majority of collections (i.e., the combined volumes of the virtual library) are no longer locally held. On an increasing basis, acquisitions decisions are made in a statewide rather than local environment. This is as true for the bibliographer as for the library director. Increasingly, the success of OhioLINK depends upon one primary factor—the degree to which the local library can integrate into the larger context to solve traditional problems. OhioLINK has radically redefined the terms of library cooperation. Closely related to the theme of "cooperation at the core" is the theme of an outward vision or focus.

OUTWARD VISION

Cooperation cannot succeed with an exclusive focus on local needs. The importance of an outward vision, under the rubric of "libraries without walls," has been discussed openly for at least a decade. In practice, this is a radical concept. In Ohio, many want a "library without walls," as long as it doesn't affect the local library.

A good example of this conflict is the replacement of local cataloging with outsourcing at Wright State University. Those preoccupied with the local library insist that local cataloging is important. Yet the founding of the Online Computer Library Center (OCLC) began a logical progression based on an outward vision leading to the Wright State decision. The purpose of OCLC is to eliminate duplication of effort by hundreds, even thousands, of catalogers in local libraries. Based on the overwhelming success of shared cataloging, it is logical to purchase the bibliographic record with the book. The national attention, much of it negative, created by the Wright State decision, however, is more than catalogers worried about jobs; it is a continued and inappropriate focus on the local library.

Similar to traditional cataloging yielding to new realities and solutions, the overburdened interlibrary loan process must also be transformed. Again, solutions will be found in the environment external to the local library, the local constituency, and the parent institution.

THE INVISIBLE USER

The vanishing patron, or invisible user, is both a fear and reality of the rapidly advancing electronic environment. At the University of Cincinnati, however, a steady increase in the number of patrons entering the library building is reality. On the other hand, there is a significant and growing number of individuals remotely accessing the library catalog and electronic databases. While many do both, we know we will increasingly interact with our patrons electronically rather than in person.

Based on the financial necessity of expanding cooperative activity, the need to plan through an outward vision, and the reality of the invisible patron, the service function must change. Namely, change must occur in collection development, reference service, and library instruction.

COLLECTION DEVELOPMENT

In most academic and public libraries, collection development is a function of reference bibliographers or branch department heads. Their task requires a shift from building stand-alone local collections to developing contributions to a larger, virtual collection. This changing emphasis on collection development requires new tasks for the bibliographer:

1. *Actively and consciously create a virtual collection strategy.* The virtual collection exists as a concept rather than a local physical reality. The development of the collection is based on the needs of the faculty and students and not on the "completeness" of coverage of every subject area. Needs are not met only through local ownership but through the "virtual collection" consisting of interlibrary loan, regional consortia, and commercial vendors. The task of the bibliographer is to "map" the virtual collection and identify and construct appropriate external resources.

2. *Shift development efforts from the local collection to regional, state, and national consortia.* The local collection can no longer be the primary focus of attention. Bibliographers must have increased involvement in cooperative collection development, cancellation projects, conspectus projects, and the establishment of commercial information services and collection sharing agreements. Such efforts already exist in Illinois, Ohio, Louisiana, Colorado, and Iowa in addition to the activities of the Committee on Institutional Cooperation (CIC).

3. *Increase bibliographers' sophistication in dealing with format and technological infrastructure.* Microforms, CD-ROMs, online catalogs, videotapes, tape cassettes, and music compact discs all require a sophisticated knowledge of hardware infrastructure. The bibliographer must relate format to the mediating technology to make wise and useful collection development decisions.

4. *Increase the bibliographers' sophistication in dealing with a wide variety of financial arrangements.* The electronic environment provides a plethora of financial arrangements including traditional purchasing, leasing CD-ROM products, reselling items like FirstSearch, and licensing databases. Bibliographers must consequently understand the vagaries of possible contracts and how they fit local and state requirements. They must be able to identify varying levels of service and have the ability to begin the negotiation process. This is particularly important because multiple financial options exist for most products, and, in many cases, similar or overlapping products have a range of financial options. The selector must determine which options and/or products are the most cost-

effective, given the expected patterns of use by patrons. It may make more sense to buy information by the article through the UnCover Company or pay the additional cost of a site license for a product requiring heavy use needed in multiple locations.

REFERENCE SERVICES

Reference librarians have legitimately become very skeptical about new roles in the electronic environment. Invariably, it means more work in a week that already goes well beyond 40 hours. Consequently, the roles of the reference librarian should not be increased but transformed. We must, therefore, do the following:

1. *Eliminate the traditional reference desk based on in-person mediation as the primary vehicle for providing intellectual access to library resources.* Reference librarians will be most reluctant to forego this interaction with patrons. It is necessary, however, because traditional reference service is incredibly expensive. No other profession waits around to be useful whenever needed. More to the point, reference librarians are overworked and overwhelmed at present staffing levels. Providing enough reference librarians to do the job adequately is financially impossible. In addition, reference librarians have created reference collections designed for reference librarians and not library patrons. We take the books out of call number order and arrange them in idiosyncratic ways in the reference area and wonder why patrons ask for help in using the materials. This is self-propagation. A cost-effective and practical solution is to place paraprofessionals at the desk with reference assistance available only on a scheduled or referred basis as pioneered at Iowa State University and the University of Cincinnati.

2. *Focus professional reference expertise and skills on providing better systems rather than on solving individual problems.* Reference librarians have traditionally provided ambulance service at the bottom of the cliff rather than construct fences at the top of the cliff. This is a perversion of the service ethic of a devoted reference staff. We must correct systemic problems such as poor signage, bad physical layout, and inadequately designed catalogs instead of relying on reference librarians to solve problems patron-by-patron.

LIBRARY INSTRUCTION

As compared to "one-at-a-time" instruction at the reference desk, bibliographic, or library, instruction is extremely cost-effective in that many students are served simultaneously. It is no longer necessary for the librarian to provide mediation between patron and information. The electronic revolution is eroding the need for and importance of such personal mediation. This is being replaced with new instructional tasks for the public services librarian. There are three key elements in the development of a viable library instruction program:

1. *Instruction, not traditional reference, is the primary method librarians should use to provide intellectual access to the collection.* Reference and information-desk services are ancillary to basic instruction. Library instruction must replace traditional reference service as the primary means of providing intellectual access to the collection. Expensive, highly trained reference librarians are not trained to handle intense, group-oriented instruction. Instead, a separate library instruction department should be established independent of the reference unit. The new unit should report directly to an associate dean or director. This independence is necessary because it is often difficult for reference librarians to view the reallocation of resources as productive. Unfortunately, change is regarded as cannibalization of resources and interference with the traditional mission.

Patrons no longer insist that a reference librarian answer queries for them. As technology becomes less exotic and information systems become more convenient and easy to use, patrons increasingly want to do it themselves. One example is chemistry departments owning passwords to Chemical Abstracts Services (CAS) because it is more convenient to conduct research on a personal schedule rather than waiting for a reference librarian. A second example is OhioLINK's patron-initiated circulation system, which is faster and more convenient than traditional interlibrary loan. It operates 24 hours a day, does not require a visit to the library, and involves no complicated forms.

2. *Instruction should be developed as a curriculum, not a series of independent sessions.* Librarians converse easily about traditional reference services; the success of the reference interview; and the distinction between directional, informational, and reference questions. Librarians are only now beginning to develop a language and tradition of instruction, including a dialogue about curricular issues. A curriculum is a defined body of knowledge presented in a series of integrated, interrelated courses. A library instruction curriculum should consist of courses provided in a logical sequence, grounded in basics proceeded by more advanced concepts. There should be a logical relationship among all courses to insure that all important information is covered and inappropriate duplication and repetition is avoided.

3. *Library instruction should be supplemented through the development of access tools to facilitate independent library use.* The failure of the library profession to design effective and highly interactive information systems necessitated the use of reference librarians. Similar to emergency room personnel in a hospital, we forget to practice preventive medicine rather than develop and refine emergency procedures.

Librarians must design user-friendly tools that can be employed easily by independent patrons. The interactive nature of the electronic environment allows unprecedented opportunities for success. Examples include help screens, particularly those that are contextually sensitive; sophisticated tutorials and front-ends such as *Reference Manager* or Ohio State University's *Gateway*; Innovative

Interfaces, Inc. (III) embedded Gopher with "hot links" from MARC records to reviews, full text, and other online tools.

As such tools are developed, librarians must remember that navigating vast collections of electronic data as well as evaluating found information is equal in importance to information access. The electronic environment has been so successful in providing information that we must protect patrons from becoming overwhelmed and intimidated. Public service librarians must take responsibility for insuring that databases and other tools are productive and effective and add substantial value to the learning experience.

CONCLUSION

The traditional library is well on the way to becoming a very different type of institution. The electronic environment encourages and mandates fundamental changes in how patrons' needs are met. While the local institution will not disappear, it will be increasingly defined through participation in the larger, virtual library. Success in this arena, particularly among public service personnel, requires an outward focus, a willingness to radically redefine cooperation, an awareness of the invisibility of patrons, and an appreciation of increasingly complex funding mechanisms.

In this period of rapid and dramatic change, we must reorganize what should *not* change. The underlying mission of libraries is the preservation of and provision of access to the important documents of the human record. This represents an ancient, honorable, and unchanging mission of at least 3,000 years. Strategies for accomplishing this mission change naturally and regularly. Traditional methodologies, such as reference-desk services and AACR2 cataloging are being replaced by more appropriate and effective technologies. With an open mind, librarians must freely examine mechanisms for achievement of an unchanging mission in an environment of rapid change.

10

Technical Services in the Revolutionized Environment

William A. Gosling

As the quantity of information expands and the electronic media for its delivery proliferates, libraries of all types are being challenged to provide facile access in response to reader demands. The more common CD-ROM and online reference sources are now often joined by access to large files of marked-up full-text, digital images, multimedia, and massive data sets. In addition, with computer desktop publishing, there is an explosion of soft publishing and distribution via the Internet not experienced a few years ago. Libraries, in response to this proliferation of formats, are challenged to assist readers in identifying what they want from this mass of information and how best to deliver it or provide remote access at the desktop. Technical services operations are changing to facilitate this access by providing new means of information structure and manipulation beyond traditional "bibliographic control."

A first challenge is to identify what should be described in the library's online catalog and what of the new formats may be self-indexing. How can the mass of information generated be evaluated and selected, and how can appropriate descriptions and pointers be provided for those materials that warrant such treatment?

Technical services operations are feeling the effects of the rapidly changing technology and the challenges and opportunities that these electronic formats present. Major forces, within and without the library, are dictating migration to newer, more efficient methods of handling services to provide sophisticated access to electronic information for the ever more demanding user population. A variety of collaborative projects is launching a second conversion, from print to digitized collections, following the earlier conversion of catalog records. Publishers of journals are on the threshold of issuing their new publications in electronic format.

One is particularly challenged in this dynamic environment to describe current technical services operations, let alone trying to create a snapshot of what may evolve in the next several years. How will the electronic environment alter technical services and the tasks and operations required of library staff? A major factor certainly will be the rate of change that is occurring in our society and the workplace today, reflected in the development of a wide array of new electronic tools and formats for information resources offered through both traditional commercial sources and the publishing being created or accessed through desktop connections to the Internet.

HISTORICAL PERSPECTIVE

Before looking ahead, however, it is useful to reflect back over the past century during which librarianship has been in a continuous state of transition, although at a less rapid and noticeable pace than the current rate of change. Gradual transition (the process of changing from one form, state, activity, or place to another) has been occurring in libraries throughout this century. A couple of examples will suffice to illustrate that this change is something library staff have effectively incorporated into their work procedures on a regular basis.

Remember when circulation procedures required that you turn the pencil so that you could use the date stamp affixed to the eraser end and then turn it around to write the patron's name on the charge slip, which had to be filed manually? Later, staff typed the overdue notices. Eventually, barcodes were applied, and staff learned to use the barcode reader. Today, circulation procedures are greatly improved through automated systems that expedite the charging, record keeping, and preparing of overdue notices. The fundamental tasks remain the same while the tools and processes have greatly improved, enabling patron self-charging in some libraries.

Most staff do not remember in-house card production routines in which a master card was written in the *library hand.* With the availability of typewriters, cards were typed locally, a card set was printed, and the red ribbon was activated in the typewriter for over-typing the subject headings. This process evolved from (1) using locally produced card masters to (2) using Library of Congress generated card sets to (3) using OCLC, RLIN, and other utilities for card production. With the advent of the online catalog, procedures gradually changed to machine-based systems that accept tape transfer of MARC records. Libraries now are beginning to use File Transfer Protocol (FTP) to move bibliographic and authority records into and out of local systems and the network electronically. Who, today, would want to return to the expense of creating manual records and filing them into and maintaining a manual card catalog?

There are many other examples of change in preservation, acquisitions, and related areas of traditional library service. These two examples suffice to illustrate the operational changes that have occurred to provide added value to library services, enhancements that, for the most part, have been created by staff or adapted to local applications to serve users more efficiently. Even that concept has changed. No longer are there *users*; they have become customers or clientele in today's total quality management setting.

What would library work be like today in relation to the rest of society if staff were not employing fax machines and personal computers (PCs), accessing remote information resources and electronic databases over the Internet, and using electronic mail or remote access to online catalogs? We would be sadly out-of-date and out of the mainstream of modern information delivery systems. But libraries are very much in the forefront of these developments, adopting and adapting to each new development as it expands the ability to provide information resources to an ever-larger global audience.

TECHNICAL SERVICES ORGANIZATIONAL CHANGES

As change agents, technical service librarians are part of this contemporary transition process. Selection of electronic materials means that staff are incorporating new formats of materials into library collections and supporting operations, are providing bibliographic descriptions of these newer formats, and are using computerized tools essential to expedite that work. Before looking at some of the operational changes occurring in the 1990s, it is useful first to look at alterations to the organizational structure, many of which have occurred in the last two to four years and contributed to the rate and variety of change being experienced.

The Technical Services Directors of Large Research Libraries Discussion Group (Association for Library Collections and Technical Services, a division of the American Library Association) has been a forum for the discussion of topics affecting technical service operations for more than twenty years. When I first joined this group as the Duke University representative in 1976, the members had titles such as "Assistant University Librarian" or "Associate" or "Assistant Director for Technical Services." Due to recent staffing changes, members in this group now serve with titles such as "Deputy University Librarian," "Assistant Director for Technical Services and Library Systems," "Associate Director for Collections and Cataloging," "Associate University Librarian for Administrative Services," and a variety of other titles reflecting experimental patterns of institutional organization that meet the needs of an institution at the given moment but that may change as the organizational structure evolves.

In some institutions, acquisitions is merged with collections. In others, interlibrary loan operations have been moved into technical services. The traditional acquisitions, serials, and cataloging department structures often are difficult to identify. Functions are being merged, and management positions are being redefined accordingly. Organizations are being flattened; in some institutions, there is no longer an Assistant Director for Technical Services with overall responsibility for the operations that make up this segment of the library. Instead, unit managers comprise a team to oversee these activities and to coordinate contribution to national programs. This raises the question of how we will coordinate activities during the last half of the 1990s to provide the kind of broad overview that helps insure a smooth continuum throughout the processing workflow and oversees the introduction and adoption of new techniques and modernized services. To accommodate shrinking budgets and the need to reduce staffing levels, different staffing patterns are being employed, resulting in the variety of organizational models noted above. Different models appear to meet specific institutional needs of the moment rather than the generic organizational structure that was in place in most libraries during the preceding 30 years or more.

This structural change has the potential to make it more difficult to discuss today's issues owing to the lack of common areas of responsibility by those managing technical services. If the Technical Services Directors Discussion Group is reflective of this transition, however, it may produce a more informative exchange as each member brings to the table a different perspective enriching the whole. On the other hand, it may be that we have lost from our libraries a sense of the full spectrum of those operations necessary to process materials, regardless of format, and prepare them for the library's clientele. Is there still the commitment to quality bibliographic access which has been the hallmark of America's academic libraries throughout much of this century? As we move into more automated indexing systems, one is often left with the impression that our organizations value less the bibliographic record and what it has enabled us to do in the management of collections through online catalogs. Yet, discussions among colleagues designing modern systems highlight the need for these records as the metadata of broader electronic services. One also has to ask, what will serve as the training ground for future managers or directors with this change in structure?

TECHNICAL SERVICES OPERATIONS

Acquisitions

Once selected, how will materials be acquired? Some print-based titles will be purchased through traditional acquisition ordering processes while others will be acquired under growing numbers of approval plans. Other items will arrive in response to interactive online systems connected directly to the vendor's or publisher's computer, using FTP or CD-ROM for the delivery mechanism.

At the 1995 American Library Association midwinter meeting, a new service for libraries was featured by the bibliographic utilities and vendors whereby the book suppliers offer cataloging for books delivered through approval plans; this is equally applicable to firm orders. In some cases, it is based on an agreement between the book vendors and the cataloging utilities where the utility is notified when a vendor is ready to ship a group of titles; the records for these titles, embedded with local information as supplied by the vendor, can be FTP'd to the library simultaneously.

In another model, the vendor supplies from its database records with the books to facilitate processing upon receipt. The network is notified of the titles to set the library's holding symbol. The result may be an enriched record, including table of contents data and, in the near future, multiple sets of subject headings from various discipline-specific thesauri.

There also are new ways of acquiring electronic materials, bypassing traditional acquisitions in many cases altogether or requiring no acquisitions because the only acquisitions function is a note in the bibliographic record pointing to the electronic address to access the item over the Internet online. One example is the delivery of the Elsevier materials science electronic journals provided through The University Licensing Project (TULIP). Titles are transferred directly into disk storage by a technician without manual check-in or other handling. As more materials become available in this format, it will greatly reduce check-in operations. Other electronic materials require a more intensive acquisition operation as an extensive negotiation of license agreements is needed. This process will involve careful coordination with other segments of the library to support acquisition of the necessary equipment, disk storage, and software in order to provide access to the information product.

Cataloging

Creation of original records is essential if other institutions are to benefit from copy cataloging. There will continue to be a need for catalogers for both original and copy work for the foreseeable future. What they are processing, however, may shift dramatically.

It was mentioned earlier that there are many new formats being introduced into library collections or to which remote access is provided for library users. What does this encompass? These products include image files of print materials; new publications issued as large image sets, such as the Chadwyke-Healey English Poetry database and the materials science journals in the Elsevier TULIP project; full-text files; electronic serials; numeric datasets; and recently, multimedia, in addition to the wide array of video and audio cassettes, software, and CD-ROM products. One anticipates shortly that new electronic books will be brought into the bibliographic mainstream as well.

Several academic libraries are exploring the receipt of a significant proportion of new books fully processed by the vendor. A book, barcoded, labeled, and marked with identification ready for the shelf, would arrive in the library at the shelving point. Following a brief selection review (although not mandatory), the item would be ready for circulation. Locations would be supplied based on the subject matter as reflected in the approval processing profile, or vendors could tailor the records to local specifications, working within the institutional catalog if needed. It remains to be seen how effective this external source of preprocessed materials will be as a scaleable operation. Given vendors' success in providing this service to public and school libraries, it holds promise for helping eliminate work for economically strapped academic libraries.

To provide bibliographic access to these materials requires the development of new standards to describe properly the various formats and the requirements for their access and use; standards development will thus need to be expedited.

One of the challenges in trying to address this wide array of material is that traditional records, through the library's online public access catalog and the OCLC, RLIN, and other utilities, may no longer be adequate or appropriate without dynamic linkages to the electronic content itself. Further preparation of these records requires broader expertise on the part of the cataloging staff. Not only must they know the standard cataloging rules and the use of newer generic descriptor names and essential fields, such as the 856 field, they must take advantage of an exciting opportunity to become involved in shaping the electronic products created and offered through Gopher, Mosaic, and Netscape servers to open up access and usability of full-text, image, and data files.

At the University of Michigan, staff are working with a variety of products in electronic format that are challenging the technical services operation, both in providing adequate description and in preparing the material for fullest utilization by the library's clientele. The library—in parallel with several other research institutions such as the University of Virginia, Cornell, Columbia, the Rutgers–Princeton Center for Electronic Texts in the Humanities, and the University of California system—is offering full-text files of book materials. Seven original catalogers from monographic and serials cataloging units are receiving training in the Standard General Markup Language (SGML) for full-text materials. Colleagues have advised that it takes a minimum of ten hours, applying over 300 different SGML tags, to mark up a single work. While images of text can be loaded onto a server and made available without the SGML markup, they are not readily searchable, especially in a comparative manner that is so valuable to humanities researchers.

The catalogers being trained in SGML work also will prepare Text Encoding Initiative (TEI) headers which require a smaller set of approximately 50 SGML tags. As more work is accomplished in the preparation of TEI headers and as the creators of electronic texts learn more about this methodology, materials may come into the library with the headers already prepared. It is anticipated that tagged data in these headers then can be mapped over to corresponding fields in a MARC bibliographic record, enabling one process for the preparation of the descriptive information which becomes an index within the document and the OPAC access mechanism to the item in the collection. Michigan has created a Humanities Text Initiative in which staff have brought together more than

5,000 texts, including old English, middle English, and modern English works, and the Chadwyke-Healey English Poetry database, among others. These titles generally require bibliographic description, as well as SGML markup, to enable searching across the text and make them known to the researchers. One question being explored is whether records reside only in the local OPAC due to restricted licensing access for campus-use-only materials, or do they also get sent to the utilities.

Other staff are working with the Institute for Social Research's data files to provide descriptive records to enable researchers to learn of their content. Added processing steps may include providing information on how to access the data, incorporating the code books in electronic format within the data set and, where possible, eventually assisting in the creation of analysis models of respective subsets of the data.

Some colleagues argue that once the researcher gets into the respective file with proper indexing of image files and preparation of TEI headers, he/she will be able to search the file using these built-in keys without aid of OPAC records. Others argue, however, that patrons will not be able to find their way through the mass of information that will eventually be accumulated in this electronic sea any easier than they are able to find their way through the mass of materials shelved within a large research collection without the catalog to help point the way, or a modified version of it with some reasonable level of authority control. Can we assume the patron will find the correct file with all the related data sought without a centralized directional system to aid them? The several projects underway to bring bibliographic control to full-texts and Internet resources suggest cataloging records will be beneficial.

There will continue to be a need for original cataloging for both print and electronic items, at least among the largest libraries, to create records that will provide this access for researchers and possibly for other institutions. As noted in the Michigan experience above, the expansion of cataloging to handle the growing volume of electronic full-texts with SGML already is beginning, as it is at other full-text centers.

Another aspect of the electronic materials record is that it may not require copy cataloging by each institution. There may not be a local location or book number necessitating integration into the local collection. Rather, records may be bought *en* block and loaded into the local catalog with requisite pointers to the various electronic texts available for that material. Sets of image files or SGML texts may have available units of records similar to those created in the past for large microform sets, supplied by the producer of the material or by a cataloging data supplier.

Serials

In the area of serials, cooperative efforts with the Committee on Institutional Cooperation (CIC)—the Big Ten plus the University of Chicago and the University of Illinois at Chicago—are focusing on cataloging electronic serials from the Internet. They will be experimenting with creating bibliographic records that include notes describing access to the original file address, as well as the archived version available on the CICNet Gopher server. Other libraries and partnerships are working to gain control over Internet resources. The eventual result will be access through an OPAC and servers to a variety of electronic formats, eventually with electronic links so that the technical services "cataloger" will be providing direct linkage to the electronic image itself.

Electronic serials offer some exciting opportunities for providing traditional bibliographic access not only through the OPAC but via the recently created 856 field with the ability to create a Hypertext link directly to an image version of the item described in the bibliographic record. This dynamic record brings with it the need to maintain the electronic addresses to the serial image source files, especially if they are on remote servers. Mechanisms are being developed to test these addresses electronically and, if one does not function properly, to alert a system monitor when an adjustment is necessary. Such techniques will not provide information about name changes or content changes but will alert file maintenance teams of the need to adjust the address accordingly. Will this work be performed as part of the function of the catalog maintenance staff, by a public service point, within library systems, by a unit outside the library, or by some combination?

Electronic journals may be offered as image files or as fully marked-up SGML products with information encoded about title, issue, cost, and related data. These journals could be checked in automatically to the library's computer system and an authorization for payment generated, and the readers could be automatically notified of articles in that issue of interest to them. The role of the manual serial records operation is largely replaced in such a situation.

As one of the TULIP sites, the University of Michigan Library has been working closely with Karen Hunter, Vice President of Elsevier, in looking at the challenges of handling large image journal files for which storage disk space and printing capabilities are constant challenges. In a recent communication, Ms. Hunter was asked how she saw paper being replaced with the electronic medium. She replied that from her Elsevier view, it was anticipated that there will be a transition in several stages, with paper remaining the dominant carrier for the balance of the decade and probably longer. Elsevier envisions libraries working with a parallel paper and electronic set of formats. She noted that for 1995 Elsevier has 1,100 journals available in the TULIP mode as image files, as well as in print. However, the cost of adequate bandwidth to support real browsing, i.e., T3 lines, is too high for viable remote host systems, while the T1 line speed now commonly available is too slow for users. There will be a need to upgrade the local lines to T3 levels to facilitate image transmission.

Given these situations, initial electronic journal systems will be held either all locally, or through a combination of local storage for the more recent issues and the more highly used titles, with CD-ROM jukebox or remote archives utilized for the less frequently consulted items. Libraries may rely on availability through document delivery services for lesser used items. One of the questions to be addressed is, as greater bandwidth becomes available at lower costs, will there be a migration to more remote storage rather than mounting the files in each local library. Will a national periodical or an electronic journal center emerge? As an effort is made to move to SGML versions, there still will be issues of file size, scalability, print capabilities, charging mechanisms for royalties and printing, and handling of graphics, multimedia, and color, among other issues to be addressed. There is a long road ahead before the fully operational electronic serial library service is available.

To provide proper access, delivery of electronic formats assumes that libraries have in-place the appropriate equipment infrastructure for users to access the information they need, when they need it, including software and hardware. It requires that the appropriate pointers are present to direct the user to where the item is located. It also assumes there is a parallel set of equipment for staff to acquire and process new receipts, although some of the support may come through partnership support from the computing center.

Another aspect of serials is the possibility of migrating from the issue-based to the article-based journal. With standard numbering schemes to order and process them, it may be more economical to process only requested articles. This would present major changes in technical services operations to manage such a collection, although one anticipates the technology may greatly facilitate that process. Such operations involve the integration of sophisticated software to access, move, display, and print desired articles, operations with which the serials staff will need to become familiar. It is anticipated that by the end of the decade all major journals will be available in electronic as well as paper format. Given this scenario, it raises the question, among other issues within cataloging, of handling multiple formats. Should separate records be created for each variant electronic version of a unit of information or should multiple versions be applied, noting through copy holdings or other notations the various formats that may be accessed, either remotely or through in-house servers? The migration to delivering electronic serials will provide major opportunities for experimentation and learning how to manage this challenging format, including on-demand printing services.

NEW FORMATS

Efforts are underway to create large image files of print and special collection materials. These files, along with the full-text files, are in some ways like the large microform sets with which libraries have been dealing for years. Often a collection-level record is all that has been available in the catalog unless special funding for cooperative cataloging projects provided bibliographic access in the form of separate records for each title. If this is not to be repeated with the electronic files, major cooperative cataloging projects will be needed. Some of the cooperative agreements, such as the CONSER Program for Serials and the emerging Program for Cooperative Cataloging for monographs, as well as the various regional consortia working to define cooperative projects, will be important in providing the full range of analytics for the large electronic files, whether they are full-text, bitmapped image, or electronic serials.

With the possibility of direct links to the information itself, hopefully libraries can avoid some of the pitfalls of converting the card catalog to the online catalog by creating more dynamic interactive systems. In the former process, it was largely replicating information which was on the card in a machine-readable record initially. Efforts to enhance the catalog now are being tested. With online systems, it is possible to create a more dynamic linkage tool for patrons as projects are funded to convert the collections from print to a format that can be electronically manipulated. Hypertext links from bibliographic records to the electronic text through the use of the 856 field should become the norm. Libraries soon will be faced with the challenge of deciding what to provide locally versus what will be accessed remotely. In both cases, bibliographic access will be essential. For remote materials, part of the technical services operation, such as the manual recording of individual issues and the fund accounting features, will disappear. These operations may be handled electronically through file connections or by insertion of an electronic link in the existing bibliographic record.

Locally mounted files also will present a major preservation challenge. While in some libraries preservation is part of technical services, in others it is part of collections or reports directly to the senior library administrator. A recent article in the January 1995 *Scientific American* noted that most electronic materials will need to be refreshed within five years. How will we preserve the electronic materials being produced via Internet, on CD-ROM-based products, or locally online in the library?

The rate at which millions, if not billions, of images will be generated in the near future is going to provide a major challenge to all parts of the library community for description, access, preservation, and public service. In addition, the files will need to be refreshed regularly to insure their availability, especially if the original document is destroyed in creating the electronic version. Experiments with computer image to microform production, and microform conversion to image production, suggest that more work is needed, including on the policy level, to determine how best to preserve the content regardless of the format of library collections.

In terms of the organizational structure, it was mentioned earlier that the administrative level was changing and position titles were being adjusted. Other roles are changing, and exciting new staffing opportunities are emerging. Recently at Michigan, the technical services staff has been called upon to coordinate the Gopher information resources, as well as to assist in the design of the Mosaic server for the campus. Cataloging staff at both the librarian and paraprofessional levels have been asked to assist groups in the organization of information within the new electronic tools. Catalogers have received training in SGML applications, and this has quickly led to identification of the need to provide UNIX training to enable them to understand better the more technologically sophisticated environment in which they are beginning to work. They approach this work with enthusiasm and excitement. The challenge for libraries will be to maintain well-trained workforces to process the sustained flow of print material while addressing the rapidly escalating array of electronic resources and the need to provide adequate bibliographic access for both.

What does all this mean for technical services operations? In the long-term, it means that technical services will need to find more efficient ways of using the bibliographic records as they are captured or created. For electronic resources, it may be possible for selectors to identify a record in the utility and, with a simple command, pull that record into the local catalog, thereby completing the process for providing access to the material which is at a remote site. As large electronic repositories are created, either at an individual institution or through cooperatives such as CIC, cataloging staff will be called upon to help process the electronic material, which may or may not be received through traditional acquisition departments; to apply appropriate tagging for its efficient use within the library; and to work with systems and computing staff to coordinate these multiple formats to provide a uniform access mechanism for the library user.

With the growing ability to create products in a multimedia environment, information creators require assistance in how to structure and organize information. The cataloger is being recognized as a resource to provide this expertise in the organization of information. Technical services staff are beginning to work with teams across multiple disciplines, including author, computing, and library expertise, to provide the array of skills necessary to make an effective product.

Electronic formats will be delivered and processed using new methods that will alter, if not eliminate, segments of traditional technical services operations. The challenges of how to receive, store, make available, and preserve images and full-text files in a cost-effective manner will occupy all segments of the library, including technical services and library systems staff. These operations may blend more closely into shared operations. The revamped processing systems will be more automated, relying on new partners and freeing staff resources to interact more directly with the information consumer.

These trends in the creation and management of electronic information resources and their delivery to the reader require that technical services staff receive added training in the latest technologies. Libraries must find the necessary resources to hire the staff required for this type of processing work, as it may be more labor intensive than preparing bibliographic records for traditional print materials. Rather than disappearing, technical services support is taking on an expanding role, although where it resides within the organization may shift to team initiatives and multitask groups. Libraries will need to make an ongoing major investment in training staff in these new procedures, so that as the electronic information systems mature and creators gain sophistication in their production, the products will become more accessible and of greater use to the reader.

11

Strategic Planning and the Allocation of Library Resources

Gary M. Pitkin

The purpose of strategic planning is to align, realign, or maintain an alignment between the organization and the environment. Strategic planning in that context is a process of identifying the environment and developing organizational strategies that are consistent with that environment. Key performance indicators measure the health, effectiveness, and efficiencies of an organization and show how well the organization is functioning within its environment. The indicators thus have a strong relationship to the environment, are consistent with the strategies, and help monitor the success of the strategies.

Within this context of strategic planning, the University of Northern Colorado Libraries established a campuswide approach to the creation of a plan for the Library System. To help insure that the strategic plan was sympathetic to the information requirements of all constituencies, the University Libraries Unit Planning Committee was comprised of library administrators, faculty and staff, teaching faculty from every College, and graduate students. The committee began by identifying preliminary key performance indicators (KPIs). Environmental trends categorized as opportunities and threats in the external environment and strengths and weaknesses in the internal environment were then explored. A cross-impact analysis was conducted to identify those KPIs which the committee felt had a strong relationship to the environment.

MISSION AND ROLE

Prior to examining the specific key performance indicators and the strategies created to address them, it is important to understand the motivations involved. One of the major impacts of the strategic planning process was that it forced the committee to review and reestablish our mission. The previous mission statement had been produced in 1982 in preparation for the ten-year accreditation process conducted by the North Central Association. In the strategic planning process, the mission is then supported by statements of purpose or role. In an effort to represent traditional service values, the impending electronic environment, and our philosophical commitment to the concepts of virtual access and virtual libraries, the mission statement was geared toward functions of service. This was followed by role statements that moved the traditional environment into the realities of the electronic environment. The mission and role statements as defined by and in the Strategic Plan are as follows:

Mission Statement: The University of Northern Colorado Libraries form a strategic, intellectual environment for learning, research, and problem solving in the academic community. Within this academic environment, the University Libraries serve the entire range of scholarship through the selection, organization, retrieval, interpretation, and conservation of intellectual resources no matter where those resources are located. Library personnel serve as information teachers and bibliographic consultants for faculty, staff, and students in classroom situations and on a one-to-one basis. The University Libraries extend their services well beyond the campus to other academic libraries and reference centers, to public schools and public school educators, to the community, and to other public interest organizations.

Role One: *A primary role of the University Libraries is to provide access to information anywhere in any format to support the curricular and research needs of the University community.* Information that supports classroom instruction and faculty research interests is essential to scholarship in the University community. The information may be in print, non-print or electronic format. The information may be available in the collections of the UNC [University of Northern Colorado] Libraries or it may be retrieved from external library and commercial sources and learning centers around the world.

Role Two: *As the primary information provider for the University community, the Libraries serve as a leader in evaluating and applying technology for managing and providing information.* Technology is becoming a very important tool for accessing and managing information. Indexed databases are available through online catalogs, the Internet, and other electronic networks. Such databases are also available on CD-ROMs as stand-alone workstations or as part of local area networks. Documents themselves may be retrieved from full-text databases or via file transfers through the Internet and downloaded to personal computers. The University Libraries have been using technological tools to access and manage information and continue to explore applications of technology for information retrieval and management.

Role Three: *The Libraries serve as an educator to ensure that all members of the University community are information literate.* Information literacy is defined as the ability to access, understand, manipulate, and evaluate information from any source in any format. Access to information includes searching online library catalogs, electronic databases and other information resources as well as navigating electronic networks while evaluation involves comparing and contrasting information retrieved. Instruction occurs through one-on-one reference service interactions between library faculty and patrons. Another setting for instruction is the classroom. Library faculty provide bibliographic instruction/information literacy components in Freshman English and graduate research courses. Library personnel also offer Internet training programs for classroom faculty. Further cooperative efforts with college and academic department personnel are necessary to incorporate information literacy more fully into the curriculum.

ENVIRONMENTAL TRENDS

The strategic planning process requires that environmental trends that impact mission and role be identified prior to the development of KPIs and their associated strategies. The external environment is the social, political, economic, and technological context in which the organization functions. The internal environment consists of the vagaries of the parent institution and the libraries as part of that organization. The trends identified for the University of Northern Colorado Libraries are as follows:

External Environment

1. *Information is proliferating.* Information is appearing in a variety of formats besides print—micro, video, film, compact disc, electronic. The amount of information in all formats is increasing exponentially.

2. *Information technology is rapidly emerging and changing.* Online catalogs are becoming global. Stand-alone CD-ROM workstations are being incorporated into local area networks. Networks are connecting to networks in a worldwide web.

3. *Information can be accessed quickly without an intermediary.* Electronic networks such as the Internet make it possible for an individual to retrieve information directly from a variety of sources. A person does not have to wait to purchase material or borrow it from a library. Patrons can request documents or transfer files electronically.

4. *The ability to access, evaluate, and synthesize information will become increasingly important.* The information cannot be used unless it can be accessed, understood, and evaluated. In a world of proliferating information and rapidly developing technologies, the potential benefits of information increase. At the same time, utilizing that information becomes more difficult.

5. *The increasing costs of traditional information formats and the high cost of information in electronic formats limit the information resources that libraries can provide.* The rising costs of serials have forced libraries to cancel subscriptions and reduce monograph purchases. Libraries must also weigh the cost of CD-ROMs and electronic databases when making decisions about information resources.

6. *The level of government funding for higher education is expected to remain the same or decrease.* At a time when there is more information available in a variety of formats, reduced state government funding makes it more difficult for a public institution to acquire information sources. The ability to supplement state appropriations

through federal grant resources is rapidly diminishing. The challenge is to develop new models for providing information.

7. *Declining public and legislative confidence in higher education is leading to a greater emphasis on assessment and accountability.* Institutions of higher education will be expected to demonstrate that graduates have the skill necessary to be productive and to contribute to society. Those skills will include the ability to access and analyze information.

Internal Environment

1. *A campus network will enable members of the University community to access information from within and outside the University Libraries.* Access will be provided from within the Libraries as well as from university-supported labs and individual workstations outside the Libraries. The information will include that available through the Libraries and via the Internet.

2. *The University Libraries' integrated library system offers opportunities for expanding access to information.* Indexed databases and other information sources are being mounted on the Colorado Alliance of Research Libraries (CARL) system. The system also offers the potential for enhancing internal library operations.

3. *Increasing graduate and off-campus enrollments coupled with steady or declining funding will require careful management of human as well as financial resources.* The size of the staff, levels of responsibility, and job assignments will need to be evaluated on an ongoing basis to adjust to the changing information management environment and to accommodate new technologies that enhance library operations. Current sources of external funds will need to be developed further. New sources of external funding will also need to be pursued.

4. *Incoming students lack the information literacy skills to be successful in an academic environment.* Information literacy instruction programs need to reach a large number of students and cover basic to more advanced skills.

STRATEGIES

In support of the mission and role statements and in response to the identified external and internal environments, strategies were developed to provide direction for future activity. The strategies clearly indicate priorities for action developed through the strategic planning process. Those strategies are as follows:

Strategies to Maintain and Enhance Access to Information

Strategy One: Provide desktop and lab access to indexed databases and other information through existing and emerging technologies.

1. Identify and procure hardware necessary to provide access to databases and information sources from within the Libraries, university-supported labs, on-campus networked connections, and remote sites.

2. Identify and procure indexed databases that support the curricular and research needs of the university community.

3. Identify and procure noncommercial sources of information for dissemination to the university community.

Strategy Two: Provide full-text access to materials not owned by the University Libraries.

1. Identify and procure full-text databases that support the curricular and research needs of the university community.
2. Expand utilization of commercial document delivery sources including UnCover, the Online Computer Library Center, and the British Lending Library.
3. Expand utilization of interlibrary loan capabilities through the Internet and the Ariel Network.
4. Provide gateway access to Fee-based Internet and related sources that support the curricular and research needs of the university community.
5. Provide file-transfer protocol (FTP) and related services for the direct retrieval of needed documents via the Internet.

Strategy Three: Provide full-text access to high-demand materials in all formats through a local, core collection.

1. Identify and procure high-demand materials that are necessary to support the curricular and research needs of the university community.
2. Expand access to government publications and archival records in the online public-access catalog.

Strategy Four: Expand opportunities for students, faculty, and staff to become self-sufficient in the "virtual" employment of library services.

1. Enable the university community to conduct self-generated interlibrary loan, circulation, and holds placement activity from any networked, on-campus site or appropriate remote location.
2. Provide the capability for students, faculty, and staff to check out materials in the Libraries through an automated self-check system.
3. Systematically replace all "dumb" CARL terminals with personal computers to allow self-generated activity on-site and same-station access to Internet resources.

Strategy Five: Provide leadership in the state, and nationally and internationally, for the expansion of resource-sharing activities.

1. Through CARL, design cooperative collection development policies and procedures to foster the creation of a regional collection to be shared on a demand basis.
2. Develop strategies for cooperative selection and cancellation of journal titles with guaranteed access to at least one subscription within the Colorado Alliance of Research Libraries (CARL).
3. Develop policies and procedures for the creation of cooperatively designed, electronically based collections.

Strategies to Insure that all Members of the University Community are Information Literate

Strategy Six: Provide instruction to insure that all members of the university community are information literate.

1. Continue to provide, through the team-teaching approach, bibliographic information/information literacy components in freshman English and graduate research courses.
2. Plan and team-teach a full-semester course on information access at the undergraduate level.
3. Expand the Internet workshop program provided to classroom faculty by the University Libraries' faculty and Information Services personnel.
4. Continue and expand, through emerging technologies, the one-on-one teaching prac-

tice of library faculty providing information-access skills to patrons through reference service interaction.

5. Design and implement computer-based library self-paced instruction tools.

Strategy Seven: Provide facilities conducive to instructional support for information literacy.

1. Construct an Information Literacy Presentation Facility with full Ethernet, Internet, CARL, and multi-media presentation capabilities.
2. Provide adequate information literacy presentation capabilities in the Music Library and the Laboratory School Library and Media Center.

Strategies to Maintain and Enhance Service Excellence

Strategy Eight: Provide avenues of support for personnel training and development within the scope of the changing technological environment.

1. Continue to financially support the staff development program.
2. Continue to send personnel to appropriate management and technology training programs.
3. Obtain additional funding for personnel to travel for developmental purposes.
4. Increase support to all personnel through applications of information technology.

Strategy Nine: Provide the space necessary to maintain and enhance library services.

1. Relocate the Music Library to a more efficient facility.
2. Expand the main library.
3. Enhance existing space for the Laboratory School Library and Media Center.

ALIGNING FINANCIAL RESOURCES WITH THE STRATEGIC PLAN

The nine individual strategies are being accomplished through the diversion of financial resources away from traditional allocations. By concentrating on the strategies identified through the strategic planning process, the University of Northern Colorado Libraries are addressing environmental trends and, in turn, are meeting the "real" needs of its constituencies. To this end, specific projects have been funded as priorities.

In allocating dollars to address "Strategies to Maintain and Enhance Access to Information," the Libraries completed the following:

1. FirstSearch: The University Libraries installed a gateway on the CARL Public Access Catalog to allow access to FirstSearch, a product of the Online Library Computer Center. Access is provided to WORLDCAT, ARTICLE/FIRST, CONTENTS/FIRST, PROCEEDINGS/FIRST, PAPERS/FIRST, MEDLINE, ERIC, and the GOVERNMENT PRINTING OFFICE MONTHLY CATALOG.

2. Online Databases and Full-Text Journal Access: Through CARL, the Libraries purchased CDP Technologies' Ovid Software to provide public catalog access to BIOSIS, CINAHL, ERIC, HUMANITIES INDEX, MEDLINE, PSYCINFO, and the SOCIAL SCIENCES INDEX. The Libraries also converted InfoTrac from CD-ROM to the public catalog environment providing online, indexed access to 2,350 journal titles.

In addition, the Libraries implemented a pilot project to test full-text access to 1,100 InfoTrac business periodicals and the reports of 130,000 private and 20,000 public corporations.

3. THOMAS and GPO ACCESS: The Libraries established gateway access to THOMAS, the Library of Congress' hyperlink to a searchable, full-text database of all versions of all the bills of the 103rd and 104th Congresses. THOMAS also connects to the House and Senate gophers, to the Library of Congress' universal government information locator, and the CONGRESSIONAL RECORD. The Libraries also established a gateway to GPO ACCESS, the Government Printing Office's Wide-Area-Information server providing key-word, full-text access to the FEDERAL REGISTER and the CONGRESSIONAL RECORD.

"Strategies to Ensure that All Members of the University Community are Information Literate" were addressed through the following initiatives:

1. Information Literacy Presentation Facility: This is a state-of-the-art electronic classroom designed to (a) teach access to and utilization of CARL, online, and CD-ROM databases and Internet resources, and allow hands-on experience at individual workstations, (b) teach the functionality of information kiosks, and (c) conduct workshops for academic faculty on multimedia resources and classroom applications.

2. Library Escort: This is a computerized library instruction program with directional maps and photographs. Escort has three components: (a) UNC Libraries Information containing descriptions of collections, services, and policies, (b) Library Tour taking students through the various areas of the main library in a logical order for conducting library research, and (c) Research Assistant, a commercial, interactive program customized to link collections and services to students writing research papers.

And finally, the Libraries addressed "Strategies to Maintain and Enhance Service Excellence" through the following projects:

1. UNC Libraries Expressway (UNCLE): This is a simple online, menu-driven system designed to provide traditional services 24 hours a day, seven days a week. UNCLE allows patrons to electronically renew books, request interlibrary loan materials, ask reference questions, and see what new CD-ROMs the Government Publications Department has received.

2. Marcel: This is an innovative, electronic document delivery system created and designed by the University Libraries. Based on MIME-encoded (thus the name Marcel) e-mail, this system will allow patrons to request articles through Interlibrary Loan and have the required documents print in local accounts, complete with graphics and audio and video clips.

CONCLUSION

Through the strategic planning process, the Libraries of the University of Northern Colorado identified the realities of its external and internal environments. These realities were employed to completely redesign the organization's mission statement and redefine academic and support roles. Key Performance Indicators were developed in response to mission and role to formulate numerical criteria upon which strategies could be designed as priorities for the achievement of role and mission.

Based on a strong confidence in the strategic planning process and the resultant plan, the Libraries have allocated financial and personnel resources in accordance with the identified strategies. The result is an organization that is increasingly responsive to its environment, and consequently the constituencies it serves. The result is an organization that is more responsive to the needs of the university community. The result is increased visibility, a stronger political platform, and increased funding. The Libraries are working in concert with the parent institution at a greater level, and the parent institution is more supportive of the libraries as an organization. Everyone benefits.

12

Are Libraries Necessary in the Revolutionized Environment?

Robert C. Heterick, Jr.

About the turn of the century a very clever English physicist, James Clerk Maxwell, suggested a way to beat the Second Law of Thermodynamics. The Second Law has to do with entropy—the measure of the unavailability of useful energy in a system when that system is left to fend for itself.

Maxwell's thought experiment was to imagine a demon at a trap door of a divider in the middle of a container filled with gas at a constant temperature and pressure. The demon would observe the molecules bouncing around and would judiciously open and close the trap door to permit the faster molecules into one side of the container and the slower into the other. Over time, one side would get hotter and the other colder, organizing the latent heat energy and thereby overturning the Second Law of Thermodynamics.

Most modern enterprises have introduced just such a demon into their management philosophy, organizational structure, products, and services. That demon is the array of digital technologies unleashed by the integrated circuit and fiber optics. The physical embodiment of the demon is millions of personal computers and workstations connected by millions of miles of fiber optic cable undergirding a global telecommunications system. The current incorporeal manifestation ranges from simulations and industrial robots through electronic data interchange to the World Wide Web.

Libraries, not unlike many other old and established enterprises, are asking themselves if there is a place for them in this new electronic environment and, if so, how will this demon impact them.

My experience has primarily been with academic research libraries and these comments are heavily influenced by that experience. It seems to me, however, that the same set of external forces are confronting libraries of all types and that the response of libraries to the computer and telecommunications revolution, from small public to large research, will be similar.

We should probably begin by noting that our current paper-based collections aren't going away. We might further observe that, by any measure, the amount of nonpaper material that might form part of library collections is currently very small and growing noticeably, but slowly. Clearly the paper-based collections in the nation's libraries are going to continue to grow for some time. Such growth is likely to be accompanied by even more difficult resource deficiencies in our libraries, continuing the severe pressures on library acquisition policies.

The systems theorist Gerry Weinberg once postulated Prescott's Pickle Principle (Weinberg 1985: 125)—cucumbers get more pickled than the brine gets cucumbered. A small system, say libraries, operating in a much larger one, the national and world economies, will be changed as the larger system changes. The question for libraries is whether they will proactively move to shape their new future or will passively be carried along. In that sense, libraries are no different than the steel or auto industries, IBM, the regional telephone companies, or any other segment of our economy.

Some of the aforementioned examples might give us pause. Recent history suggests that most of the industrial endeavors that were passively carried along, or attempted to resist change, experienced significantly reduced market share, lost market leadership, and lost value to consumers sufficient to attack their viability. IBM is a classic example of a company not reacting to the change swirling around its markets. In spite of its size and strength it managed to lose half its stock value in an eighteen-month period as it stuck defiantly to a strategy incompatible with that change.

It is time, past time actually, for us to return to basics and ask ourselves what is, or should be, the role of libraries in the new electronic environment. Seriously asking such a question is bound to expose the extent to which our accommodations with past print technology have created a whole series of compromises. These compromises have been subtly institutionalized, making change appear much more difficult than it really need be.

At one level, one of those basics might be to make some portion of the world's information available to the populace—learners, researchers, entrepreneurs . . . the generally inquisitive. At this level, the electronic revolution should play directly into the hands of libraries. As increasing amounts of the world's stock of information become available electronically, it becomes increasingly possible to connect the inquisitive with information stripped of the temporal and geographic constraints that have for so long been a part of the accommodations with old technology.

The library as "place" is a paradigm that will need some new rationale beyond housing a paper-based collection. The card catalog, or its electronic equivalent in the MARC record, is another idea that is tied to the old technology and not well suited for the information age. Libraries must move beyond these transitional strategies that automate the old world view and discover new service implementations that add value to the patron in the electronic environment. In short, libraries must go through the same reengineering process as is corporate America.

So it would seem, to thrive in the information age, libraries will have to maintain a warehousing paradigm for an increasing amount of paper-based information while simultaneously creating a new product line—access to networked information. Libraries, like every other business of the information age, will have to put the client first and, rather than being place-, or building-, or collection-centric, will have to focus on satisfying the information needs of their clientele, wherever they may occur, whenever the need arises.

This suggests that, in the information age, navigation will become more important than collections and librarians will be more important than libraries.

PLAYING THE TRADE-OFF GAME

There is an old saying in the golf world that the woods are full of long hitters. You can hit the ball long, or you can hit the ball straight. You can't consistently hit the ball your longest and your straightest. This kind of a trade-off isn't new. Enterprises, including libraries, make it every day—serials versus monographs, collection versus staff—in literally hundreds of ways in the day-to-day conduct of business.

The new trade-off isn't between familiar alternatives, but now focuses on collection building vs. access. What's more, for certain segments of our patrons, access to networked information has taken supremacy over print collections and their numbers are growing rapidly. This is very clear in the science, technology, and medical communities where current awareness information that has historically been the province of the scholarly journal is rapidly moving to the network. Increasingly, the network is becoming the preferred medium for the distribution of the latest in scientific discovery. We see the same phenomena in the business world, where the "typed" letter is preceded by a facsimile copy, or dispensed with altogether in favor of electronic mail or some form of electronic data interchange.

The "just-in-case" strategy that held sway in an era of paper collections will give way to a "just-in-time" approach for electronically accessible material. The relative value attached to libraries based upon collection size will rapidly dissipate during the next decade. In the electronic environment, the size of all libraries' collections will be the same. It may well turn out that smaller public libraries will have an easier time making the transition required by the electronic revolution as they will be relatively unencumbered by a large historic collection of print material.

The rise of multimedia, in both electronic mail and Web pages, is sure to exacerbate this move from the printed page and long lead times to instantaneous "publishing" of text, video, and sound on the Internet. A similar trend can be observed in reference works with more static content, first on CD-ROM and eventually on the Internet. Whereas today we tend to view multimedia formats as something new, in a decade we will have begun to view print, or sound recordings, or video as special cases of a more generic "publication" that is likely to seamlessly incorporate them all.

The rapid expansion of the Internet into a national, then global, information infrastructure will obviate the need for local collections of material in electronic formats. The trade-off, in fact the guessing game for libraries, will be how fast which types of information will move from historic print formats to electronic accessibility on the Internet and what, if any, mediating role patrons will want libraries to play.

Research libraries that attempt to archive and make available the historical record of information in particular fields will be confronted with a particularly thorny problem for which there is no accepted answer. The inexorable march of technology will continue to make obsolete the formats in which multimedia material is developed and presented. Who will have a physical CD-ROM drive capable of reading 1990s CDs in 2040? And even if they did, who will have 1990s computers and operating systems that will have any hope of working in 2040, or even 2010?

This problem dwarfs the text-only problem of dealing with "dead" languages where one had to either translate the material into some current language or provide a dictionary and thesaurus for the defunct language. The close coupling of the hardware with the operating system software with the application software makes a similar translation-like solution prohibitively expensive and time consuming.

A similar problem arises in regard to both the robustness and stability of sources of information on the Internet. Will a source of information still be there next year? Or even next month? And even if it is, how will we deal with the dynamic nature of its information base which is constantly undergoing refinement and change? Will it even make sense to attempt to catalog and describe the various "editions" of such ephemeral material?

The good news, of course, is that electronic distribution of current awareness material offers the potential to remove about 40 percent of the cost—that portion that is associated with making and distributing the artifact that contains the information. It further offers the user access to that material from the desktop just about anytime and anywhere.

As the client is able to access information directly on the Internet, the public good funding model for libraries will come under additional stress. Information consumers will not need, nor generally want, the mediation of libraries in their access to current awareness information. Such access is likely to be gained under license or "pay per view" strategies. While there may be a role for libraries as license aggregators, will there be a role for lending under Fair Use in the electronic environment?

The public good funding model treats libraries as sort of a natural monopoly that provides value to citizens. That value ultimately accrues indirectly to governments as a consequence of more informed citizens or more directly in the form of greater tax revenues as a consequence of improved industry and invention. With a new and, one should observe, incredibly well-funded set of competitors (the phone and cable companies, motion picture and television studios, recording industry giants, and software houses), there clearly is not a natural monopoly, and competition for resources, whether from governments or consumers, will be fierce. The rhetoric underlying both a Democratic administration and a Republican Congress is aggressively pro-competition, private sector, when it comes to the national information infrastructure.

As governmental, and perhaps even private, enthusiasm for funding information intermediaries and providers attenuates, it is all the more necessary that libraries find ways to leverage the massive public-private investment that will be made in the national information infrastructure. Our current investment in libraries of all types will represent only noise level in the investment that will be made by the private sector in the next decade. A whole new set of value-added service opportunities will arise—license aggregators, desktop delivery, network navigation, network publishing—that could become the province of the nation's libraries as well as commercial service providers.

INTELLECTUAL PROPERTY

Intellectual property in the networked world promises to be, by far, the most difficult transition that libraries and their patrons will have to confront. The Internet was built in a public-private partnership. That partnership has yet to find a mechanism to address difficult questions of intellectual property in the information age. A copyright regime must develop that, on the one hand, provides market incentives, while on the other permits evolution of the network for public sector purposes of education, art, cultural expression, and the like.

These are not new trade-offs. However, the digital media and distribution systems are unprecedented and cannot be understood by simple extrapolation of our trade-offs designed to deal with managing copyright of print commodities. Much of our current intellectual property law has worked because the intellectual property was, perforce, packaged in an artifact of tangible dimension and heft that was expensive and difficult to copy. Too much of the debate surrounding intellectual property in the information age is focused on the short-term problem of managing text converted from print to digital format. Too little attention is directed toward the long-term issues of promoting innovation in our digital networks built upon digital forms of knowledge representation and communication.

If we are to realize the goal of a learning society, we must find a solution to dealing with intellectual property in the information age. Networked information will be the medium for renaissance in higher education and, likely, for other public sector domains as well. We need to rise above parochial group lobbying, move beyond litigation, and avoid simplistic extrapolations of legislation designed to deal with issues of an industrial age economy and a print commodity. We need to recognize that the world of the Internet will be different than any we have previously experienced. Attempts to treat print, sound, video, and software as separable issues won't work in a world of network delivered multimedia.

Digital information is nonexcludable (copying is essentially free) and nondiminishible (copying is almost perfect). A learning society will be built with derivative works and the bundling of public with private goods by value adders. Both citation and the concept of "authorship" seem to be breaking down on the Internet as we witness increased citing of the mail forwarder rather than the original author and as more and more works are collaborative in ways that seem to defy attribution of "authorship." Does anyone care? Should anyone care?

In the information age, every reader-listener-viewer may also be an author-composer-director. Without protection to the creators of intellectual property, there won't be any goods. Without a sense of balance between security and access, the public interest cannot be served. At best, the information age is a Faustian bargain for librarians and publishers. Each will have to give up something that was valued in the industrial age paradigm in order to exploit the promise of the information age. They must recognize that it is not a zero sum game and that each can profit from new treatments of intellectual property.

The intellectual property debate is confounded by our failure to differentiate between two kinds of publishing on the Internet—that done with the intention of making a profit and that done with no such intention. One could argue that in the print world, the value-add of publishers was such that all publishing was done with the intention of recovering minimally the not insignificant cost of printing and distribution. That need not be, and is not, the case of publishing electronically. Just as the Federal government through tax incentives encouraged the development of not-for-profit corporations during the trust-busting days earlier in this century, we may need a new legally recognized category of not-for-profit publishing on the Internet. We might recognize that the Internet will be populated with much information for which the authors ask no, and expect no, compensation. Such would, or could, certainly be the case for much scholarly information.

Current (1995) efforts to deal legislatively with intellectual property issues are somewhat disheartening. The so-called Green Paper produced by the Clinton administration calls for subtle, but important, changes in first sale doctrine and digital transmission and retransmission rights. Both seem as wrong-headed as the demands from net surfers that all network information be free.

Whatever mechanisms we advance to deal with the question of intellectual property in the information age, they must strike a balance between security for the copyright holder and access in the public interest. This problem can be likened to that of finding a guard dog that is mean enough to scare off burglars but sufficiently docile so as to not bite the postal carrier.

DISINTERMEDIATION AND DISAGGREGATION

The First Law of Thermodynamics observes that the amount of energy in a closed system is constant. The easiest way to make a system vibrant and robust is to connect it to even larger systems, permitting the import and export of information and energy among them. This is precisely what is happening in the Internet. And as was true with the nation's telephone system, each new network added to the Internet enhances value to all far in excess of the ratio of new connections to the old.

The Internet continues to grow at better than 10 percent per month, doubling in less than a year the number of connected networks, or computers, or users, or any other measure of size. There is still a long way to go to reach the level of ubiquity of the phone system, or even the cable television system, but penetrating 60 to 90 percent of the homes and workplaces in the United States certainly seems reasonable in the coming decade. The current, and future, growth of the Internet is primarily in commercial service providers. The Internet, and the emerging national information infrastructure, has transitioned from academic curiosity to a means of commerce.

One of the salient characteristics of all these electronic technologies has been rapid diffusion in the presence of disintermediation. The phone system languished for several decades until the invention of the crossbar switch technology and dial tone. Until that time, it was necessary to interpose a mediator, the operator, into the process of making a phone call. Dial tone disintermediated the telephone system, and its diffusion into 95 percent of the homes and workplaces essentially took place in the two decades following.

There is a significant lesson here for libraries as they map their strategic plans for the information age. Front line, user interface, mediation will be automatic—done by "smart" software. Human mediation will move one level back, much as it has done in today's telephone system. Institutions built on a mediator philosophy will not survive the information age—not only because of cost pressures but more importantly because of client preferences in using the technology.

One of the corollaries of the First Law presaged the Second Law by observing that the potential energy of a system tends to a minimum. We clearly observe this in our networked information world where, absent good navigation tools, the value of the Internet quickly is dissipated in anarchy, and its potential rapidly declines to a minimum. The World Wide Web and its Mosaic-like clients give us a taste of what opening our systems can bring. They bring, as well, a lesson in what effort will be required to maintain them.

Economists have long had their own statement of the First Law—"there ain't no such thing as a free lunch." As we struggle with the cost of growing and maintaining these networked information resources, we will find ourselves increasingly directed by the "invisible hand" of a marketplace. This will be a difficult transition for an enterprise that is one of the last hold-outs of public good socialism, and an enterprise that has been used to near monopoly control of a geographically contained service area. We will find all libraries competing with major academic research libraries, and perhaps with the Library of Congress and other national libraries not only in the United States, but all across the world. And they will be competing as well with commercial suppliers in what had been the sole province of libraries.

Another lesson of the diffusion of these electronic technologies is disaggregation and differentiation. Service suites that have been historically lumped together in the absence of competition are suddenly attacked by "cream skimmers" or niche marketeers. These niche players will identify some portion of the service suite to which they can add value or reduce costs, or sometimes both, and will compete aggressively for that portion of the service suite. The termination of the national telephone monopoly is a good case in point. It gave rise to long-distance competition, bandwidth aggregators, alternate operator services, a huge private branch exchange marketplace, and directory service publishers. The list is long and incredibly varied. While the occasional user of telephone services may sometimes lament the loss of focus from a single service provider, savvy users greet the niche players with enthusiasm as they drive down costs and, through innovation, provide services not heretofore available.

Disaggregation will clearly extend to the "bundling" of information products. The bundling of disparate articles into journals will sooner, rather than later, fall prey to disaggregation. The vestiges of long lead times, scheduled publication dates, and perhaps even prepublication review will quickly disappear as disaggregated "chunks" of information become the norm on the Internet.

The process of service disaggregation brings with it differentiation. It reinforces the means rather than ends of the service and causes the industrial age "one size fits all" service model to falter and eventually fail. Systems designed to deliver aggregated services in cost-effective ways fall prey to service differentiators who find new and unexpected uses for old services.

This will be an exceedingly difficult transition for libraries. In the absence of monopoly, competition always drives out cross subsidies. As libraries' monopoly status erodes, the rationale for internal cross subsidies (efforts to be "efficient" in the aggregate) will come under increasing attack. As a consequence, it will be more and more difficult to view the library service suite holistically.

THE DIGITAL LIBRARY

Murphy, that clever pessimist, once observed that "left to themselves, things always go from bad to worse." This, of course, is just a restatement of the Second Law of Thermodynamics. The question we should probably be asking ourselves is not "Are libraries necessary in the electronic environment?" but rather, "What will libraries do to avoid the slow, cold death consequent to the Second Law?"

Leaving aside the archival and special collections aspect of many of the nation's libraries, there are still many roles that libraries might play in our electronic future. We might try to discern what they are and ask if libraries, as historically constituted or ultimately transformed by the demon, are best positioned to do them.

It is ironic that libraries, whose methods and procedures have brought so much order to our print heritage, appear so noticeably neglectful in devising strategies for doing the same with our electronic future. One wonders if libraries are getting more and more specialized in dealing with our print-based past so that they will provide everything for nobody, while the Internet is more and more anarchic so that it provides nothing for everybody.

Attempts to force-fit the MARC record to our multimedia future already show signs of failure. As more and more nonprint-based material from sources such as museums become available on the Net, the shortcomings of the MARC record, itself a transliteration from the card catalog, are increasingly apparent. Our network-finding mechanisms—WAIS and Archie, for instance—are not the work of professional librarians but rather the fledgling efforts of computer scientists.

Cataloging of our electronic resources must recognize the dynamic, as opposed to static, nature of the material. It must be prepared to cope with the multimedia aspects of the material. And it needs to recognize that the material will be spread around the nation and the world as a matter of course.

We have long been aware of the Square Law of Complexity—the complexity of a system increases at least as fast as the square of the number of tightly coupled components. It is this law that helps us understand why we can't build hugely complex centralized software systems, and why distributing the intelligence decouples the relations, thereby reducing the intellectual and computational labor necessary to understand and build them. This, of course, is precisely what Sir Isaac Newton did when he reduced the study of the motions of heavenly bodies to the simple interaction between the sun and each planet. And it is why client-server systems will supplant centralized systems, why centralized phone switches will give way to Internet-like distributed systems, and why centralized collections will fall prey to electronic resources distributed worldwide.

Libraries, and more particularly librarians, may take this problem as their own. But if they do not claim it, and quickly, it will be taken by others intent on solving the navigation problems of the Internet. The window of opportunity for librarians to claim this issue is rapidly closing. It is worth noting that industrial age standards processes aren't working in the information age. Rather than lengthy (years and decades) standards debates, the world of the Internet operates on short "try it and if you like it, use it" processes. It is interesting (and informative) that none of the major network tools, the World Wide Web, Mosaic, WAIS, and Gopher, evolved from a typical standards process.

It seems likely that organizational/hierarchical strategies in libraries will be less important than devising new collaborations between librarians and information technologists and between both and their users. Many libraries have prided themselves on their insularity and their vertical integration that permitted them to operate with minimal interaction with outside agencies. In the electronic environment, libraries must learn to define themselves in terms of the communities they serve. Libraries have a recent, rich history of collaboration among themselves—Online Computer Library Center, Research Libraries Information Network, Inter-Library Loan—but the collaborations needed for the future are with patrons more than with other libraries.

Library patrons are using the technologies of computing and communications to reengineer their businesses. The successful library in the electronic environment will devise strategies to complement the reengineering efforts of their patrons. As the patrons' style of using information changes, library services must change, and they must change in anticipation of patron preferences.

In the new world of the Internet, libraries will need to pay particular attention to their funding mechanisms. As disintermediation and disaggregation encourage funding shifts from providers to consumers, and as deficit situations at all levels of government encourage significant reductions in funding discretionary budget items, libraries will need to look for new and innovative funding sources. Absent such new strategies, as the *ALA Goal 2000* (ALA 1995) report observed, libraries run the risk of "being pushed to the periphery."

One phenomenon that bears watching by libraries is the rise of community information utilities. These entities represent new opportunities for collaboration as well as new sources of funding. They may well become the information age version of Yellow Pages that are interactive and multimedia. They provide the opportunity for libraries to expand their service suites into network publishing, navigational aids, electronic "collection development," and a host of new, patron-oriented services.

Libraries have a role in the emerging electronic environment that extends beyond serving as a repository for our print-based heritage or as the network access mechanism of last resort. That role will become clearer as they develop the demon that permits them to develop new strategies to deal with cataloging, navigation, collaboration, and funding issues. If they do it well, and quickly, they will be leaders in the emerging electronic environment as they have been in our print-based past. One lesson libraries, in fact all enterprises, need to learn from the First Law is its alternative statement that "there is no such thing as a perpetual motion machine." No matter what the enterprise's level of accomplishment in the industrial age, it will need to prove itself anew in the information age. Failure to rethink, reengineer, and reinvent the enterprise in times of great change will certainly lead to the cold death predicted by the Second Law.

REFERENCES

American Library Association. 1995. *ALA Goal 2000*. Chicago: American Library Association.

Weinberg, Gerald M. 1985. *The Secrets of Consulting*. New York: Dorset House Publishing.

Selected
Bibliography

Abraham, W. V. 1983. "Inheritance and Style: Planning Design at Macquarie University." *Planning for Higher Education* 11: 1–9.

American Library Association. 1994. Telecommunications and Information Infrastructure Policy Forum. "Principles for the Development of the National Information Infrastructure." (brochure)

American Library Association. 1995. *ALA Goal 2000.* Chicago: American Library Association.

Association of American Universities, AAU Task Force on Intellectual Property Rights. 1994. *Report of the AAU Task Force on Intellectual Property Rights in an Electronic Environment.* Unpublished document, endorsed by AAU presidents (April 4).

Association of Research Libraries. 1994. *Reports of the AAU Task Forces on Intellectual Property Rights in an Electronic Environment.* Washington, DC: Association of Research Libraries.

Association of Research Libraries, Research Collections Committee. 1994. *Draft Strategic Plan.* Unpublished document (October 19).

Astin, Alexander. 1993. *What Matters in Colleges?* San Francisco: Jossey-Bass.

Atkins, Stephen E. 1991. *The Academic Library in the American University.* Chicago: American Library Association.

Atkinson, Ross. 1992. "The Acquisitions Librarian as Change Agent in the Transition to the Electronic Library." *Library Resources and Technical Services* 36, no. 1 (January): 7–20.

Auger, Brian. 1994–1995. "Virtual Reference Service in the D.C. Area." *The Crab: The Maryland Library Association Newsletter* 25 (Winter): 6.

Bailey, C. W. 1993. "Public Access Computer Systems." *Information Technology and Libraries* 12: 99–106.

Baird, Marcia, and Mavis Monson. 1992. "Distance Education: Meeting Diverse Learners' Needs in a Changing World." *Distance Education* 51: 65–75.

Baker, Nicholson. 1994. "Annals of Scholarship: Discards." *New Yorker* 70 (April 4): 64–86.

Baker, Shirley, and Mary Jackson. 1993. *Maximizing Access, Minimizing Cost: A First Step Toward the Information Access Future.* Washington, DC: Association of Research Libraries.

Baker, Warren J., and Arthur S. Gloster, II. 1994. "Moving Towards the Virtual University: A Vision of Technology in Higher Education." *Cause/Effect* 17, no. 2 (Summer): 4–11.

Barone, Carole A. 1989. "Planning and the Changing Role of the CIO in Higher Education." *Information Management Review* 5: 23–31.

Basch, Reva. 1994. "The 24-Hour Library." *Searcher* (September): 34–39.

Battin, Patricia. 1989. "New Ways of Thinking About Financing Information Services." In *Organizing and Managing Resources on Campus*, ed. Brian L. Hawkins. McKinney, TX: Academic Computing Publications, p. 382.

Bazillion, Richard J., and Sue Scott. 1991. "Building a High-Tech Library in a Period of Austerity." *Canadian Library Journal* 48: 393–397.

Becker, William E., and Darrell R. Lewis, eds. 1992. *The Economics of Higher Education.* Boston: Kluwer Academic Publishers.

Beckman, Margaret. 1987. "The Changing Library Environment: Requisites for Accommodating Change." *Library Hi Tech* 5, no. 20: 89–91.

Billington, James H. 1994. "The Librarian's Remarks at the National Digital Library News Conference." *Library of Congress Information Bulletin* 53, no. 20: 412–413, 416.

Billington, James H. 1994. "Electronic Content and Civilization's Discontent." In *Technologies for the 21st Century: Content and Communication*, ed. Martin Greenberger. Santa Monica, CA: Council for Technology and the Individual.

Billington, James H. 1995. "The Library and the Information Superhighway." *Civilization* (January/February): 89.

Bishoff, Liz. 1994. "Does Organizational Networking Have a Future in a Competitive Environment?" *American Libraries* (December): 990–991.

Blegen, John. 1993. "Virtual Libraries, Real Cooperation: A View of the Coalition for Networked Information." *Illinois Libraries* 75: 247–250.

Borman, Stu. 1993. "Advances in Publishing Herald Changes for Scientists." *C&EN* (June 14): 10–24.

Bowers, John. 1995. "Wiring Dixie." *NetGuide* 2 (January): 48–53.

Brindley, Lynne, ed. 1989. *The Electronic Campus: An Information Strategy.* Cambridge, England: Cambridge University Press.

Browning, John. 1993. "Libraries without Walls for Books without Pages." *Wired* 1: 62.

Butler, Brett. 1992. "Electronic Editions of Serials: The Virtual Library Model." *Serials Review* 18: 102–106.

Callan, Patrick M. 1986. *Environmental Scanning for Strategic Leadership.* San Francisco: Jossey-Bass.

Campbell, Jerry D. 1993. "Choosing to Have a Future." *American Libraries* 24 (June): 560–566.

Carter, Richard B., Sree Nilakanta, and Daniel Norris. 1991. "Strategic Planning for Information Systems: The Evidence from a Successful Implementation in an Academic Setting." *Journal on Computing Research in Education* 24: 280–288.

Case Western Reserve University. 1992. *Kelvin Smith Library, the Electronic Learning Environment Transforming Access to Knowledge: A Program Statement.* Cleveland: Case Western Reserve University.

Center for Civic Networking. 1993. *A National Strategy for Civic Networking: A Vision of Change.* Washington, DC: Center for Civic Networking.

Chronicle of Higher Education. 1994. *The Almanac.* Washington, DC.

Copyright Policy Task Force of the Triangle Research Libraries Network. 1993. *Model University Policy Regarding Faculty Publication in Scientific and Technical Journals.* Chapel Hill: Sunsite.unc.edu.

Corbin, John. 1988. "The Education of Librarians in an Age of Information Technology." *Computing, Electronic Publishing and Information Technology.* New York: Haworth Press.

Corbin, Roberta A. 1991. "Development of the National Research Education Network." *Information Technology and Libraries* 10: 212–220.

Cummings, A. M., M. L. Witee, W. G. Bowen, L. O. Lazarus, and R. H. Ekman. 1992. *University Libraries and Scholarly Communication.* Washington, DC: Association of Research Libraries for the Andrew W. Mellon Foundation.

Cummings, Anthony M. et al. 1992. *What Presidents Need to Know about the Future of University Libraries: Technology and Scholarly Communication.* Washington, DC: Association of Research Libraries.

Dahlgren, Anders C. 1989. "Designing the Flexible Small Library." *Library Hi Tech* 5, no. 20: 78–82.

Dede, Christopher J. 1992. "The Future of Multimedia: Bridging to Virtual Worlds." *Educational Technology* (May): 54–60.

Demas, Samuel. 1994. "Collection Development for the Electronic Library: A Conceptual and Organizational Model." *Library Hi Tech* 12, no. 3: 71–80.

DiMattia, Ernest A., Jr. 1993. "Total Quality Management and Servicing Users through Remote Access Technology." *The Electronic Library* 11, no. 3: 187–191.

Dougherty, R. M., and C. Hughes. 1991. *Preferred Library Futures.* Mountain View, CA: Research Library Group.

Dougherty, Richard M. 1988. "Research Library Networks: Leveraging the Benefits." *Academe* (July/August): 22–25.

Dougherty, Richard M., and Carol Hughes. 1991. *Preferred Futures for Libraries: A Summary of Six Workshops with University Provosts and Library Directors.* Mountain View, CA: Research Library Group.

Dougherty, Richard M., and Carol Hughes. 1993. *Preferred Library Futures II: Charting the Paths.* Mountain View, California: Research Library Group.

Dowlin, Kenneth E. 1993. "The Neographic Library: A 30 Year Perspective on Public Libraries." In *Libraries and the Future: Essays on the Library in the Twenty-First Century,* ed. F. W. Lancaster. New York: Haworth Press, pp. 29–43.

Drabenstott, Karen M. 1993. *Analytical Review of the Library of the Future.* Washington, DC: Council on Library Resources.

Drucker, Peter F. 1994. "The Age of Social Transformation." *The Atlantic Monthly* (November): 53–80.

Ehrmann, S. C. 1992. "Challenging the Ideal of Campus-Bound Education." *Educom Review* 27, no. 2: 22–26.

Fisher, Tom. 1995. "Impact of Computer Technology on Library Expansions." *Library Administration and Management* 9: 31–36.

Fjermedal, Grant. 1995. "The Tomorrow Makers." *NetGuide* 2 (January): 55–67.

Foote, Shelby. 1994. "Writers at Work: How Libraries Shape the Muse." *American Libraries* (December): 984.

Fox, Edward A. et al. 1991. "Users, User Interfaces, and Objects: Envision, a Digital Library." *Journal of the American Society for Information Science* 44: 480–491.

Fradkin, Bernard, and W. Lee Hisel. 1993. "Harnessing the Future: Administrative Support for Learning Resources." *Community College Journal* 63: 24–29.

Frank, Allan R., and Schuyler R. Lesher. 1991. "Planning for Executive Information Systems in Higher Education." *Cause/Effect* 14: 31–39.

Galvin, Tom. "Librarians and Campus Leadership." Informal talk given at the University of Northern Colorado, 1978. Not recorded or published.

Garrett, John. 1993. "Digital Libraries: The Grand Challenges." *Educom Review* 28: 17–21.

Gaughan, Tom. 1995. "ALA Goal 2000: Planning for the Millenium." *American Libraries* 26 (January): 17–21.

Geffert, Bryn. 1993. "Community Networks in Libraries: A Case Study of the Freenet P.A.T.H." *Public Libraries* 32 (March/April): 91–99.

Gibbs, W. Wayt. 1994. "Software's Chronic Crisis." *Scientific American* (September): 86–95.

Gorman, Michael. 1991. "The Academic Library in the Year 2001: Dream or Nightmare or Something in Between." *Journal of Academic Libraries* 17: 4–9.

Greer, Roger C. 1982. "Information Transfer: A Conceptual Model for Librarianship, Information Science and Information Management." *IATUL Proceedings* 20: 3–10.

Greer, Roger C. 1987. "A Model for the Discipline of Information Science." In *Intellectual Foundations for Information Professionals*, ed. H. Achleitner. Boulder, CO: Social Science Monographs, pp. 3–25.

Greer, Roger, and Robert Grover. 1994. "Libraries as Public Information Utilities: An Imperative for Survival." Unpublished document.

Grycz, Czeslaw J. 1992. "Economic Models for Networked Information." *Serials Review* (Spring and Summer): 11–18.

Guskin, Alan. 1994a. "Reducing Student Costs and Enhancing Student Learning. Part I." *Change* 26: 23–29.

Guskin, Alan. 1994b. "Reducing Student Costs and Enhancing Student Learning. Part II." *Change* 26: 16–25.

Hafner, Katie. 1995. "Wiring the Ivory Tower." *Newsweek* (January 30): 62–63, 66.

Handy, Charles B. 1989. *The Age of Unreason*. Boston: Harvard University Press.

Handy, Charles B. 1993. *Understanding Organizations*. New York: Oxford University Press.

Harder, E. Ruth. 1995. "Library Automation's Effect on the Interior Design of California Public Libraries." *Advances in Library Administration and Management*, vol. 13. Greenwich, CT: JAI Press.

Hardesty, Larry, and Collette Mak. 1994. "Searching for the Holy Grail: A Core Collection for Undergraduate Libraries." *The Journal of Academic Librarianship* 19: 362–371.

Hawkins, Brian L. 1994a. "Creating the Library of the Future: Incrementalism Won't Get Us There!" *Serials Librarian* 24, no. 3/4: 17–47.

Hawkins, Brian L. 1994b. "Planning for the National Electronic Library." *Educom Review* 29: 19–29.

Heath, Fred M. 1993. "The Emerging National Information Infrastructure: An Interview with Paul Evan Peters and Jim Neal." *Library Administration and Management* 7: 200–207.

Helsel, Sandra. 1992. "Virtual Reality and Education." *Educational Technology* (May): 38–42.

Herring, James E. 1987. "The Electronic School Library." *The Electronic Library* 5, no. 4 (August): 230–236.

Heterick, Robert C. 1991. "Academic Sacred Cows and Exponential Growth." *Cause/Effect* 14: 9–14.

Heterick, Robert C, Jr., and John Gehl. 1995. "Information Technology and the Year 2020." *Educom Review* (January/February): 23–25.

Heydinger, Richard B. 1994. "A Reinvented Model for Higher Education." Horizons listserv, Wednesday, September 21, 10:23 CST. Morrison@gibbs.oit.unc.edu.

Higher Education Resource Alliance of ARL, CAUSE, and EDUCOM. 1994. *What Presidents Need to Know . . . about the AAU Action Agenda for University Libraries, HEIRAlliance Executive Strategies Report #5.* Boulder, CO: CAUSE.

Hirshon, Arnold, ed. 1993. *After the Electronic Revolution, Will You Be the First to Go?* Chicago: American Library Association.

Hudson, Kathy. 1987. "Historic Buildings and Modern Technology: The California State Library Remodels for Automation—a Case Study." *Library Hi Tech* 5, no. 20: 49–57.

Hunter, Karen. 1992. "The National Site License Model." *Serials Review* 18, no. 1–2 (Spring and Summer): 71–91.

Jackson, Joab. 1995. "The Mad Librarian." *Baltimore* 88 (January): 49–50.

Jajko, Pamela. 1993. "Planning the Virtual Library." *Medical Reference Services Quarterly* 12, no. 3: 51–67.

Jensen, Robert E. 1993. "The Technology of the Future Is Already Here." *Academe* 79: 8–13.

Kane, John D., and Sharon K. B. Wright. 1993. "A National Electronic Library for Youth Development." *Journal of Agricultural and Food Information* 1: 3–19.

Kaser, David. 1987. "Designing New Space: Some New Realities." *Library Hi Tech* 5, no. 20: 87–89.

"Keeping Libraries Alive." 1994. *The Economist* 332 (August 27): 14.

Kelsey, Donald G. 1987. "Designing Space: Confronting Conflicting Demands." *Library Hi Tech* 5, no. 20: 92–94.

Kilmann, Ralph H., and Teresa J. Covin. 1988. "Preface." In *Corporate Transformation: Revitalizing Organizations for a Competitive World*, ed. Ralph H. Kilmann and Teresa J. Covin. San Francisco: Jossey-Bass.

King, Hanna. 1993. "Walls Around the Electronic Library." *Electronic Library* 11: 165–174.

Klobas, Jane E. 1990. "Managing Technological Change in Libraries and Information Services." *The Electronic Library* 8, no. 5 (October): 344–349.

Kurshan, Barbara L., Marcia A. Harrington, and Peter G. Milbury. 1994. *An Educator's Guide to Electronic Networking: Creating Virtual Communities*. Syracuse, NY: ERIC Clearinghouse on Information & Technology, Syracuse University, IR-96.

Lancaster, F. W. 1993. *Libraries and the Future: Essays on the Library in the Twenty-First Century*. New York: Haworth Press.

Library of Congress. 1994. *Strategic Directions Toward a Digital Library*. Washington, DC: Library of Congress.

Lipnack, Jessica, and Jeffrey Stamps. 1994. *The Age of the Network: Organizing Principles for the 21st Century*. Essex Junction, VT: Oliver Wight Publications.

Louis, Kenneth R. R. Gross. 1991. "The Real Costs and Financial Challenges of Library Networking: Part I." In *Networks, Open Access and Virtual Libraries: Implications for the Research Library*. Urbana-Champaign: University of Illinois Press, pp. 118–131.

Lowry, Anita. 1994. "The Information Arcade, University of Iowa Libraries." In *Managing Information Technology as a Catalyst of Change: Proceedings of the 1993 CAUSE Annual Conference, December 7–10, San Diego, California*. Boulder, CO: CAUSE.

Lucker, Jay. 1987. "Adapting Libraries to Current and Future Needs." *Library Hi Tech* 5, no. 20: 85–87.

Luskin, Bernard J. 1994. "Some Dreams and Realities for the Digital Highway." Dinner Address, Denver, CO, September 25.

Lyle, Guy R. 1963. *The President, the Professor and the College Library*. New York: H. W. Wilson.

Lynch, Clifford A. 1991. "The Development of Electronic Publishing and Digital Library Collections on the NREN." *Electronic Networking* 1: 6–22.

Malinconico, S. Michael. 1991. "Technology and the Academic Workplace." *Library Administration and Management* (Winter): 25–28.

Malinconico, S. Michael. 1992. "What Librarians Need to Know to Survive in an Age of Technology." *Journal of Education for Library and Information Science* 33, no. 3 (Summer): 226–240.

Markoff, John. 1995. "Will Video Game Machines Turn into PC Killers?" *The New York Times* (January 8): F7.

Massy, William F. 1989. *A Strategy for Productivity Improvement in College and University Academic Departments*. Palo Alto, CA: Stanford Institute for Higher Education Research.

McClure, Charles. 1992. "The High Performance Computing Act of 1991: Moving Forward." *Electronic Networking* 2: 2–10.

McClure, Charles R. et al. 1993. "Toward a Virtual Library: Internet and the National Research and Education Network." In *The Bowker Annual*. New Providence, NJ: R. R. Bowker, pp. 25–45.

McClure, Polly Ann, and James G. Williams. 1992. "Metamorphosis in Computing Services at Indiana University." *Cause/Effect* 15: 15–25.

McGill, Michael E., and John W. Slocum, Jr. 1994. *The Smarter Organization*. New York: John Wiley and Sons, Inc.

McMahon, Suzanne et al., eds. 1992. *If We Build It: Scholarly Communications and Networking Technologies: Proceedings of the North American Serials Interest Group, Inc.* New York: Haworth Press.

Michaels, David Leroy. 1987. "Technology's Impact on Library Interior Planning." *Library Hi Tech* 5, no. 20: 59–63.

Miller, R. Bruce, and Milton T. Wolf. 1992. *Thinking Robots, An Aware Internet, and Cyberpunk Librarians*. Chicago: American Library Association.

Minter, John. 1994. *Management Ratios #8, Statistical Norms for College and University*. Boulder, CO: John Minter Associates.

Montgomery County (Maryland) Department of Public Libraries. 1984. *Policy on Basic and Fee-Based Services*. Rockville, MD: Montgomery County Government.

Montgomery County (Maryland) Department of Public Libraries. 1995. *Creating a Vision for the Future: Strategic Plan for Public Libraries in Montgomery County, Maryland, FY 1996–2001*. Rockville, MD: Montgomery County Government.

Moore, Michael G. 1993. "Is Teaching Like Flying? A Total Systems View of Distance Education." *The American Journal of Distance Education* 7: 1–10.

Murr, Lawrence E., and James B. Williams. 1987. "The Roles of the Future Library." *Library Hi Tech* 5, no. 20: 7–21.

Natale, Joe. 1991. "Full and Equal Access: Americans with Disabilities Act." *Illinois Libraries* 73: 599–602.

National Center for Education Statistics. 1994. *Digest of Education Statistics, 1994*. Washington, DC: U.S. Department of Education.

Nouvel, Jean. 1990. "Centre National de la Recherche Scientifique (CNRS) Documentation Center." *GA Document* 27: 46.

Novak, Gloria. 1987. "Toward a Forgiving Building: Technical Issues Relevant to New and Existing Libraries." *Library Hi Tech* 5, no. 20: 94–99.

OCLC. 1987. *Campus of the Future: Conference on Information Resources*. Dublin, OH: OCLC.

Ottervik, Eric V., and Anthony L. Corallo. 1984. "Integrative Planning for a New Library/Computing Center." *Planning for Higher Education* 12: 15–25.

Payne, David E., Faye N. Vowell, and Lendley C. Black. 1991. "Assessment Approaches in Evaluation Processes." *NCA Quarterly* 66, no. 2 (Fall): 444–450.

Payne, David E., Faye N. Vowell, and Lendley C. Black. 1992. "Assessing Student Academic Achievement in the Context of the Criteria for Accreditation." *A Collection of Papers on Self-Study and Institutional Improvement, 1992*. Chicago: NCA.

Penniman, W. David. 1993. "Visions of the Future: Libraries and Librarianship for the Next Century." The Fifth Nasser Sharify Lecture, Sunday, April 18. New York: Pratt Graduate School of Information and Library Science. (booklet)

Peters, Thomas. 1983. *In Search of Excellence*. New York: Warner Books.

Price, Kathleen. 1993. "Xanadu Revisited: Clothing the Emperor for the New Library Role in the Electronic Library Paradigm." In *Electronic Access to Information: A New Service Paradigm* (proceedings from a symposium held July 23–24, Mountain View, CA), pp. 51–58.

Rush, James E. 1993. "Technology-Driven Resource Sharing." *Bulletin of the American Society for Information Science* (June/July): 19–23.

Saunders, Laverna M., ed. 1993. *The Virtual Library: Visions and Realities*. New York: Meckler Publishing.

Schatz, Bruce R. 1994. "Electronic Libraries and Electronic Librarians: Who Does What in a National Electronic Community." In *Emerging Communities: Integrating*

    Networked Information into Library Services, ed. Ann P. Bishop. Urbana-Champaign: University of Illinois.

"The Secretary of the Interior's 'Standards for Rehabilitation.' " 1991. *Illinois Libraries*: 628–629.

Seiler, Lauren H. 1992. "The Concept of the Book in the Age of the Digital Electronic Medium." *Library Software Review* (January/February): 19–29.

Senge, Peter. 1990. *The Fifth Discipline: The Art and Practice of the Learning Organization*. New York: Doubleday.

Shaughnessy, Thomas W. 1992. "Approaches to Developing Competencies in Research Libraries." *Library Trends* 41: 282–298.

Shirato, Linda, ed. 1992. *Working with Faculty in the New Electronic Library*. Ann Arbor, MI: Pierian Press.

Snyder, David Pearce. 1994. "Comments on the Draft Strategic Plan for Public Libraries." Paper submitted to the director of the Montgomery County Department of Public Libraries, November 30.

Sprague, Mary W. 1994. "Information-Seeking Patterns of University Administrators and Nonfaculty Professional Staff Members." *Journal of Academic Librarianship* 19: 378–383.

Steele, Colin. 1993. "Millennial Libraries: Management Changes in an Electronic Environment." *The Electronic Library* 11, no. 6: 393–402.

Tapscott, Don, and Art Caston. 1993. *Paradigm Shift: The New Promise of Information Technology*. New York: McGraw-Hill.

Taubes, Gary. 1993. "Publication by Electronic Mail Takes Physics by Storm." *Science* 259 (February 26): 1246–1248.

Telecommunications Policy Roundtable. 1994. *Renewing the Commitment to a Public Interest Telecommunications Policy: Public Interest Principles*. Washington, DC: Telecommunications Policy Roundtable. (leaflet)

Twigg, Carol A. 1994a. "Navigating the Transition." *Educom Review* 29, no. 6: 20–24.

Twigg, Carol A. 1994b. "The Need for a National Learning Infrastructure." *Educom Review* 29: 17–25.

Van Houwelin, Douglas E. 1993. "Knowledge Services in the Digitized World: Possibilities and Strategies." In *Electronic Access to Information: A New Service Paradigm* (proceedings from a symposium held July 23–24, Mountain View, CA), pp. 5–16.

Van Houwelin, Douglas E., and Michael J. McGill. 1993. *The Evolving National Information Network: Background and Challenges*. Washington, DC: The Commissions of Preservation and Access.

Vondran, Raymond F. 1990. "Rethinking Library Education in the Information Age." *Library Education and Employer Expectations*. New York: Haworth Press.

Ward, David. 1994. "Technology and the Changing Boundaries of Higher Education." *Educom Review* 29: 23–27.

Weinberg, Gerald M. 1985. *The Secrets of Consulting*. New York: Dorset House Publishing.

Young, Peter R. 1994. "Changing Information Access Economics: New Role for Libraries and Librarians." *Information Technologies and Libraries* 13 (June): 103–114.

Young, Peter R., and Jane Williams. 1994. "Libraries and the National Information Infrastructure." In *The Bowker Annual*. New Providence, NJ: R. R. Bowker, pp. 33–49.

Index

About the Contributors

KARYLE S. BUTCHER is Associate University Librarian for Public and Reference Services at Oregon State University.

ALAN N. CHARNES is Executive Director of the Colorado Alliance of Research Libraries.

WILLIAM A. GOSLING is Assistant Director for Technical Services and Systems at the University of Michigan.

AGNES M. GRIFFEN is Director of the Montgomery County (Maryland) Department of Public Libraries.

CRAIG HARTMAN is a Design Partner and Head of the Architecture Studio at Skidmore, Owings & Merrill in San Francisco.

ROBERT C. HETERICK, JR., is President of EDUCOM.

JOY REED HUGHES is Associate Provost for Information Services at Oregon State University.

DAVID F. KOHL is Dean and University Librarian at the University of Cincinnati.

CHERYL PARKER is a Staff Planner with the architectural firm Skidmore, Owings & Merrill in San Francisco.

JOHN PARMAN is an Associate of the architectural firm Skidmore, Owings & Merrill in San Francisco.

THOMAS M. PEISCHL is Dean of Academic Information Services at Northern Michigan University.

GARY M. PITKIN is Dean of University Libraries at the University of Northern Colorado.

JOHANNAH SHERRER is Director of Libraries at Lewis and Clark College.

FAYE N. VOWELL is Dean of the School of Library and Information Management at Emporia State University, Kansas.

DELMUS E. WILLIAMS is Dean of University Libraries at the University of Akron.